Almost Instant Winemaking

The Foremost Home Winemaking Series

General Editor **B. C. A. Turner**
author of *The Winemaker's Companion*

T. Edwin Belt

Almost Instant Winemaking

Mills & Boon LIMITED, LONDON
in association with
Home Beer and Winemaking

First published in Great Britain 1973 by
Mills & Boon Limited, 17–19 Foley Street, London W1A 1DR

ISBN 0 263 05372 6

Made and printed in Great Britain by
C. Nicholls & Company Ltd,
The Philips Park Press, Manchester M11 4AU

Contents

Introduction

It has been said that more wine is spoilt by being kept in the cellar too long than by being imbibed in an immature condition. Whatever the merits of the case, this is not a mistake which is likely to be made by the winemaker using this book as a guide.

It is a fact, however, that a good quality wine takes a few months to make, and requires a year or two in which to mature. Our aim herein is to make our wines within 2 to 3 weeks, by quick and easy methods, for drinking within a month, using quick-maturation techniques, and thereby to enjoy Vin Ordinaire quality in quantity.

The number of grape derivatives on the market, designed to make winemaking quicker and easier, is increasing all the time, and a growing number of food products, of increasing variety will readily serve the same purpose, given an insight into their possibilities. Certain types of wild and garden produce are also well suited to the production of almost-instant wines.

Beginners are invariably impatient to sample the results of their efforts, and if the truth be told, experienced winemakers are no less impatient, but they have the advantage of a full wine cellar to fall back upon as a curb to this curiosity. The wines described in this book are specifically designed for early drinking, and their quality should be no less than that of a reasonably priced commercial Vin Ordinaire.

All the wines described herein, being of this standard, can be enjoyed by all the family, but a quick and easy method of boosting their alcoholic content for their more convivial enjoyment on adult social occasions is also described.

This is mostly a book of recipes, since the quick and easy methods of winemaking which are described do not need detailed explanation, even to the beginner. The winemaking ingredients which are used should be available from shops near your home, and will go straight into your fermentation vessel for an immediate start on their conversion into wine. You may use the simplest of equipment, or make a few modest purchases directed towards the goal of earlier drinking of your wines.

May you make a good choice towards becoming a slim, happy and contented regular wine-bibber. Wine, as opposed to beer, is non-fattening, as I am sure you will be glad to be reminded.

1 Equipment

Most of the essential equipment required for
Vin Ordinaire winemaking will be found
amongst your kitchen utensils. We will be
describing the production of one-gallon batches,
since each recipe will then provide you with six
bottles of wine – sufficient for your household
and friends to conduct a wine-tasting
assessment of each type which appeals to you.

The equipment listed as "desirable" will speed
up the production of the wines described
herein, but the recipes, and more particularly the
methods given, are specifically designed towards
this end.

Essential Equipment:

Weighing-out Scales
Can opener
Saucepan, aluminium, 7 pint
Wide-mouthed pint bottle and cottonwool plug
Bucket, plastic, 2-gallon (Two)
Butter Muslin, sheet 2 ft square (Two)
Long-handled Plastic Spoon
Nylon Filter Bag
Funnel, plastic
Fermentation Jar, one-gallon
Fermentation Lock and Bored Rubber Bung
Tube, clear plastic, $\frac{1}{4}$ in bore
Wine Bottles, Corks and Mallet
Measuring Jug
Corkscrew

Desirable Equipment:

Hydrometer and Jar
Electric Fermentation Pad, or
Immersion Heater preset at 75°F (24°C)
Immersion Heater preset at 70°F (21°C)
Immersion Heater preset at 91°F (33°C)
Beer Mashing Immersion Heater preset at 151°F (66°C)
Holed Polystyrene Ceiling Tile for heaters
Immersion Thermometer
Filter Bag, Canvas
Wine Filtration Apparatus
Measuring cylinder (ccs) (Hydrometer Jar)
Glass U-bend for plastic tube
Plastic Tap for plastic tube
Corking Gun
Winebottle Labels
Decanter

All this equipment, except the saucepan, should
be sterilised before use by immersion in, or
swilling the inside with a solution made up of
¾ oz sodium metabisulphite and 2 oz citric acid
in half a gallon of water. Swirl the solution
around in the fermentation jar and in the bottles,
and allow to drip-dry. If the citric acid and 24
Campden tablets are used, remember that these
suffer from exposure to light and air.

Do not use a chipped enamel saucepan, or the
acids used in winemaking may react with the
exposed metal and give an off-taste to the
finished wine.

It is useful to mark the translucent plastic
bucket on the outside at the one-gallon mark;
fill the fermentation jar with water and empty it
into the bucket, when the water level can be
marked.

A large elastic band fitting tightly around the top of the bucket is useful, or a suitable length of string will serve. This is for holding the square of butter muslin on the top of the bucket on the few occasions when we will need to strain the contents of the bucket into the fermentation jar, via a second bucket.

You can buy a nylon filter bag if you so wish, but a well-boiled length of nylon stocking or tights leg will serve the same purpose, but make sure that any dye which is not fast is completely boiled out.

The liquid passes through the funnel at a much quicker rate when a gap is arranged between the leg of the funnel and the neck of the fermentation jar.

The fermentation lock provides a seal from the air by means of a few drops of tapwater, preferably in which a small fragment of a Campden tablet has been dissolved. Rubber is preferable to cork for the bung, since it is long-lasting.

When using the plastic tube to syphon the contents of one vessel into another, place the top of the receiving vessel at a lower level than the bottom of the full vessel, put one end of the tube halfway down in the liquid, then suck on the other end of the tube to start the syphon, and quickly put that end into the receiving vessel, down to the bottom. As the flow proceeds, gradually lower the end of the tube into the top vessel, and make sure that no sediment is allowed to enter the tube; the glass U-bend is designed to prevent this happening. A plastic tap on the discharge end of the tube is useful when syphoning single-handed; a plastic

clothes peg can also be used to hold the tube
at the neck of the fermentation jar.

Use brown or green bottles for red wines, and
clear glass bottles for white wines. Brown
coloured fermentation jars are also available,
by the use of which the colour of your wines is
protected from the effects of daylight. A sheet of
brown paper, wrapped around a clear-glass
fermentation jar, will serve the same purpose, or
you may be keeping your jars in a warm
cupboard, where daylight does not penetrate to
any marked degree.

A hydrometer will tell you how much sugar, for
conversion into alcohol, is present in your
dissolved ingredients; a table of sugar content
relating to any given hydrometer reading is
usually supplied with this handy instrument.
It will also tell you when a fermentation has run
its full course, and all the available sugar has
been converted into alcohol. We will generally
aim at 2 lb of natural and added sugar for total
content.

Immersion heaters can be bought preset to the
required temperatures, or you can make the
necessary adjustment to one yourself. The top
fermentation temperature of 91°F (33°C) is for
use with Tokay yeast only, when your
fermentation of red wines will be completed
within 14 days, and often less. Ordinary wine
yeast is killed at 100°F (38°C); this yeast is best
used, for our purpose, at 75°F (24°C) for red
wines, and 70°F (21°C) for white wines, when
your fermentations will be complete well within
21 days. The beer mashing immersion heater
provides a temperature level sufficient to
inactivate enzymes after their work is done, and
when boiling of the ingredients is not advisable.

An immersion thermometer is very useful for determining whether the temperature of your dissolved ingredients is low enough to enable you to introduce the yeast without fear of its being killed.

The use of a wine filter can do much to add sparkling clarity to your wines after the use of finings.

The measuring cylinder (hydrometer jar) is useful for measuring of ccs., as an alternative to fl ozs, and is sometimes needed to give an adequate depth of liquid for use with the hydrometer, which must float.

A corking gun will save you a lot of time when getting the corks into the wine bottles, otherwise a mallet must serve this purpose. The corks are well soaked in Campden solution (one Campden tablet in $\frac{1}{2}$ pint of water) before being driven home.

You'll possibly possess a corkscrew, but there are some on the market today which extract a winebottle cork without damage, trouble, or the use of strength – if yours is not the type which sits snugly over the neck of the bottle, and involves only a few clockwise turns of one screw to insert the spiral prong, and a few clockwise turns of another screw to remove the cork, then you may be giving yourself some unnecessary trouble in this essential task.

It is the modern practice to decant all wines, white as well as red, and this presents the opportunity to taste your wine and to add sugar syrup sweetening, if desired.

2 Method

STANDARD

It is a good idea to boil all the water used for winemaking. You thereby make it sterile, and thus avoid trouble from contamination; any chlorine in the tapwater is boiled away, thus avoiding its damaging effect on yeast; and finally, any "temporary hardness" is also removed by boiling, to give you a better-tasting wine.

You can, of course, just crush a yeast tablet and sprinkle it over the ingredients contained in your fermentation bucket, but in order to ensure a prompt start by the yeast on its work of rapid fermentation, we will invariably prepare a yeast starter, or in other words, we start the yeast fermenting in a wide-mouthed pint bottle, using a good yeast food, and lightly bunging the neck with cottonwool. Swill it around in the bottle occasionally, and it will be frothing up nicely on the second or third day, when it is added to the contents of your fermentation bucket. The ingredients required are:

Malt Extract, 1 tablespoonful
Citric Acid, 1 saltspoonful
Sugar, 1 dessertspoonful
Water, $\frac{1}{2}$ pint

Bring the water briefly to the boil in a small pan, after having stirred in the sugar and malt extract. Cool to lukewarm, or 75°F (24°C), or if using a Tokay yeast to 91°F (33°C), stir in the

citric acid and the yeast tablet, and funnel into
the bottle. Lightly bung the neck of the bottle
with cottonwool, to keep out the vinegar fly.
Remember that ordinary yeast is killed at
temperatures above 100°F (38°C). Keep as near as
possible to the required temperature,
dependant upon the facilities which you have
available, but whatever the temperature, try to
ensure that fluctuations do not occur; a warm
cupboard will serve our purpose. Yeast becomes
dormant at 40°F (5°C) and below, so give it
special attention during the winter months, or it
may cease to produce alcohol for you.

Any preparation of the ingredients which may
be required before the yeast starter is added to
them in the primary fermentation bucket, will be
described under each recipe. The temperature of
these liquid ingredients must not exceed those
mentioned previously when the yeast or yeast
starter is added to them – lukewarm is the nearest
description for the benefit of anyone without
an immersion thermometer.

You can, of course, stir the sugar (which is
required in practically all the recipes) into the
liquid ingredients, but a much quicker start to
fermentation will be gained if you use invert
sugar. You can buy this sugar if you so wish,
but it is a comparatively simple matter to make
your own. Pour into a saucepan the weight of
white household granulated sugar which is given
in the recipe, and for each pound in weight add
one saltspoonful of citric acid, just cover with
water, and simmer for 15 minutes, when the
liquor will be straw-coloured, indicating that you
now have a solution of invert sugar. If you buy
your invert sugar, you'll need 1¼ lb for every
pound of household sugar given in the recipes.

Whenever tannin is included in the recipe, this is provided by scalding a teabag with a pint of water, covering and leaving to brew for 10 minutes, followed by cooling; the amount of this stock solution to use is given in the recipes. A proprietary wine tannin can be used to the makers' instructions, if so desired.

Pour the yeast starter over the cool ingredients in the bucket, and keep as near as possible at the required temperature, as described for the yeast starter. Keep the bucket covered with one of the sheets of muslin, and stir twice daily for 3 days, until the initial, often violent fermentation has spent its force. If you haven't used a yeast starter, this fermentation may last for 6 days.

If there are any solid ingredients in the bucket, these must be strained out. Fasten one of the sheets of butter muslin over the top of the other bucket by means of the elastic band or string, and pour the well-stirred contents of the first bucket onto the muslin, so that the solids are retained and the liquid pours through.

Now funnel this liquid into the fermentation jar, top up, if necessary, with boiled and cooled water to the bottom of the neck, fit the bung and fermentation lock, and put some water in the lock, together with a fragment of a Campden tablet. Keep the contents of the jar as near as possible to 70°F (21°C) for white wines, 75°F (24°C) for red wines, and 91°F (33°C) when Tokay yeast is being used. A warm cupboard, or the appropriate item of equipment which has been described, will serve this purpose. Swirl the contents of the jar around daily, and make sure that water is always present in the lock sufficient to maintain the seal.

When the bubbles through the fermentation lock
become very infrequent, taste a little of the
embryo wine, and if there are no signs of
sweetness, all the sugar has been converted into
alcohol, and your fermentation is complete. The
hydrometer gives a sure indication of when this
stage has been reached, as will be described
later, but as any remaining yeast is now killed,
its use is desirable (thus ensuring that the end
product is a dry wine) but not essential. This
action is taken to make sure that the finished wine
does not recommence fermenting when it is in
the bottle, otherwise the danger and mess of
burst bottles cannot be discounted, although a
blown cork, together with spilt and spoilt wine, is
the more usual outcome in such cases.

Syphon off the wine from the fermentation jar
into a bucket, making sure that none of the
sediment at the bottom of the jar enters the
bucket, and then funnel the wine back into the
washed-out fermentation jar. Dissolve two
Campden tablets in a little boiled and cooled
water, and funnel into the fermentation jar.
Top up with boiled and cooled water to the neck
of the jar, and refit the bung and partly
water-filled lock. Swirl the contents around in
the jar daily, and keep in a very cool place, such
as a larder or cellar.

   After 24 hours, if by any chance the wine is not
clear enough for your liking, either use
proprietary wine finings to the maker's
instructions, or thoroughly beat the white of a
very small egg into a little of the wine, and return
this mixture to the fermentation jar, refitting the
partly water-filled lock, and giving the contents a
good swirl around.

Syphon the clear wine into a bucket, and stir in

$\frac{1}{2}$ fl oz (one tablespoonful) of glycerine for
light-bodied wines, and one fluid ounce for heavy
wines, or add a proprietary maturing agent to the
maker's instructions. Funnel the wine into the
bottles, filling to within $\frac{1}{2}$ in of the bottom of the
cork, drive the water-softened corks (one
Campden tablet in $\frac{1}{2}$ pint water) home with a
mallet, and store in a cool place. Label and date
the bottles.

You can be sipping your wine seven days after
bottling it.

SUPRA-STANDARD

Apart from boiling the water which you use for
winemaking, it is worthwhile to remove the
"permanent hardness" also. Your local Water
Board Engineer will send you an analysis of
the district's tapwater on request, and this will be
expressed either as ppm (parts per million) or
degrees Clarke of "permanent hardness". To
convert degrees Clarke to ppm, multiply by 14.4.
A saltspoonful, or to be more exact, 1.5 gramme
of sodium bicarbonate will remove 200 ppm of
"permanent hardness" from one gallon of your
tapwater.

The yeast starter will be prepared as previously
described, but you may well wish to ensure the
minimum of delay in the introduction of it to your
fermentation bucket, when you will keep it on your
electric fermentation pad, or you can stand it in
a bucket of water in which your immersion heater
is immersed, and thereby keep it at the correct
temperature.

Any preparation of the ingredients for your wine
is described under each recipe.

Convert the required amount of white household sugar into invert sugar, as has been described.

Prepare the tea solution as has been described or use a proprietary wine tannin to the maker's instructions, or if none given, use in the proportion of one teaspoonful per pint of tea given in the recipe.

Pour the yeast starter over the ingredients in the bucket, and insert the preset immersion heater through a hole cut in the polystyrene ceiling tile, so that it reaches to the bottom of the bucket, and switch on. Stir twice daily for 3 days, or until the fermentation has quietened sufficiently for transference to the fermentation jar without the risk of its frothing through the fermentation lock.

If there are any solid ingredients in the bucket, these are now strained out, as previously described.

Funnel the liquid into the fermentation jar, allowing a full cascade for red wines, but for white wines it is best to arrange the funnel in the neck of the jar so that the liquid runs down the inside of the jar, rather than free-falling direct to the bottom. Top up, if necessary, as previously described. The rubber bung, and fermentation lock partly filled with Campden solution, are now fitted to the jar. If the bung has a second hole to receive an immersion heater, this is also fitted, but you have at least two more optional ways of keeping the contents of the jar at the correct temperature. One method is by means of a fermentation pad, and the other is to immerse the jar in water in a bucket, and introduce an immersion heater into the bucket.

The required temperatures have been given
previously. Swirl the contents of the jar around
daily, and ensure that there is always sufficient
water in the fermentation lock.

When the bubbles through the fermentation lock
become very infrequent, take a hydrometer
reading; if this is 1.005 or less, then the embryo
wine is ready for stabilisation and maturation.

Syphon off the wine into a bucket, leaving the
sediment behind, and then funnel it back into the
clean fermentation jar. Top up with boiled and
cooled water in which 2 Campden tablets have
been dissolved, or you can use one or two
teaspoonsful of a proprietary wine stabiliser.
Refit the bung and lock. Swirl around daily, and
keep the wine cool, as previously described.

After 24 hours, if you're not satisfied with the
clarity of your wine, put a teaspoonful each of a
proprietary filter medium and of filter powder
into a bucket, and gradually add the wine,
stirring all the time. Hang a canvas filter bag
over the other bucket, and pour the wine into
the bag. You can repeat this filtering, if
necessary, until the wine is finally clear and
brilliant. A quicker method of doing this is to use
a proprietary wine filter apparatus, but this is
best used as a final treatment for absolutely
sparkling clarity, since its speed of action will be
lost if it is given too much work to do.

Stir in the glycerine or proprietary maturing
agent, as previously described, and then funnel
the wine into the bottles to within $1\frac{3}{4}$ in of the
top of the bottle. Soak the corks in previously
boiled water, or in Campden solution (one tablet
in a tumbler of water), and then use a

proprietary corking gun to drive them home.
An aluminium foil or plastic capsule is advisable,
to protect the cork from contamination. It is
helpful to label and date the bottles. Store in a
cool place.

Most people prefer a dry wine, but when a sweet
wine is called for, add a level teaspoonful of
household sugar to a half-pint glassful of the
wine, stir to dissolve, taste, and add more sugar
if not sweet enough, to taste. If it is too sweet,
you can put it into the decanter and add the
unsweetened wine, to taste. It is helpful to know
that the glassful holds 10 fl oz, and a winebottle
holds 26.6 fl oz. Diabetic sugar can be used if
required.

When drinking sparkling wines, they are best
cooled in the refrigerator before being
de-corked. The gas will then rise in attractive
bubbles from your glass, rather than in a frothy
burst from the bottle.

Red wines, generally speaking, are most
enjoyable at room temperature, whereas white
wines are best served cool.

The Table Wine recipes that follow are for full
strength wines. The same applies to the
Aperitif Wines, which are also used for making
the essence type Liqueurs, ensuring, when
formulating the recipes, that these wines are of
fully adequate body. The social wines are of table
wine strength, so that they can be enjoyed by
all the family, but there are methods of increasing
their alcoholic content for those special
occasions on which the breathalyser test does
not have to be taken into consideration; the same
remarks apply to our dessert wine formulations.

Social wines can be fortified to full strength by pouring 65 ccs (2½ fl oz) of 100° proof Vodka into a winebottle, and filling up with 690 ccs (24 fl oz) of the wine to be fortified, or alternatively, by using 45 ccs (1½ fl oz) of 140° proof Vodka and filling up with 710 ccs (25 fl oz) of the wine. Your hydrometer jar will give the more accurate cubic centimetre measures.

Dessert wines can be fortified to full strength by pouring 110 ccs (4 fl oz) of 100° proof Vodka into a winebottle, and filling up with 645 ccs (22½ fl oz) of the wine to be fortified, or alternatively, by using 75 ccs (2¾ fl oz) of 140° proof Vodka and filling up with 680 ccs (23¾ fl oz) of the wine. Once again a hydrometer jar is to be preferred, so that you can use the more accurate cubic centimetre measures.

3 Recipes

SOCIAL WINES – for entertaining friends

Aniseed

Ingredients
Aniseed 1½ oz
Teabags 8
Honey 2½ lb
Citric acid 1 dessertspoonful
Yeast nutrient 1 tablet
3 mg vitamin B1 tablet
G.P. Wine yeast 1 tablet
Water to 1 gal

Method
Simmer the honey for 15 minutes after stirring
it into the water to prevent burning. Pour it onto
the aniseed and teabags contained in a bucket.
Cool to 75°F (24°C), remove the teabags, and
stir in the other ingredients, including the yeast
starter prepared 2 days previously, and make up
to one gallon with boiled and cooled water.
Cover, and keep at the given temperature for
3 days, stirring daily, then funnel into the
fermentation jar, fit the airlock, and maintain the
temperature.

Apple Juice

Ingredients
Apple juice 29.7 fl oz can
Sugar 2 lb
Citric acid 1 teaspoonful

Yeast nutrient 1 tablet
3 mg vitamin B1 tablet
Sauterne yeast 1 tablet
Pectozyme 1 saltspoonful
Fungal amylase 1 pinch
Water to 1 gal

Method
Invert the sugar and prepare the yeast starter.
Put a Campden tablet into the apple juice when
pouring into the bucket, stir in the acid, the
pectozyme and amylase, cover, and leave at
room temperature for 24 hours. Bring briefly to
boiling point in a pan, or preferably, use a beer
mashing immersion heater to 151°F (66°C)
immersed in the bucket, (to avoid spoilation of
the taste), cool to 70°F (21°C), and stir in the
inverted sugar, nutrient, vitamin tablet, the yeast
starter, and water to one gallon. Ferment in the
covered bucket at the given temperature for 3
days, then funnel into the fermentation jar, fit
the airlock, and maintain the temperature.

Balm

Ingredients
Balm, dried, 4 oz
Red grape concentrate ½ pint
Cream of Tartar ½ oz
Sugar 1½ lb
Tea ¼ pint
Yeast nutrient 1 tablet
3 mg vitamin B1 tablet
G.P. wine yeast 1 tablet
Water to 1 gal

Method
Invert the sugar, and prepare the yeast starter
and the tea. Put the herb into a nylon filter bag

closed at both ends, and pour boiling water onto
it in a bucket; remove the bag after 15 minutes.
Cover, and leave to cool to 75°F (24°C). Stir in
the rest of the ingredients, including the
inverted sugar and the yeast starter, make up to
one gallon with boiled and cooled water, cover,
and keep at the given temperature for 3 days,
stirring daily. Funnel into a fermentation jar,
fit the airlock, and maintain the temperature.

Barley

Ingredients
Concentrated barley wine 2 lb can
Sugar $\frac{1}{2}$ lb
G.P. yeast 1 tablet
Water to 1 gal

Method
Invert the sugar and prepare the yeast starter.
Simmer the extract in 4 pints of water for 15
minutes, stirring constantly while bringing to
simmering point. Pour into a bucket, cover, and
cool to 75°F (24°C). Add the inverted sugar and
the yeast starter, make up to one gallon with
boiled and cooled water, cover, and keep at the
given temperature for 3 days, skimming off the
scum daily, and stirring afterwards. Funnel into
a fermentation jar, fit the airlock, and maintain
the temperature.

Try a handful of the leaves of Basil, left for an
afternoon in the filled decanter, for evening
enjoyment, or a sprig of the flowers and/or leafy
tips of Borage, added to the wineglassful when
pouring, or an $\frac{1}{8}$ in thick slice of cucumber
floated in the wineglassful.

Black Cherry Jam

Ingredients
Low sugar black cherry jam 3½ lb
Sugar 1¼ lb
Tea ¼ pint
Pectozyme ½ teaspoonful
Citric acid 1 saltspoonful
Yeast nutrient 1 tablet
3 mg Vitamin B1 tablet
Bordeaux yeast 1 tablet
Water to 1 gal

Method
Invert the sugar, and prepare the yeast starter
and the tea. Pour boiling water onto the jam
contained in a bucket, stir to dissolve, and
strain into a second bucket. Cover and cool to
60°F (16°C), stir in the pectozyme and acid,
cover, and leave for 24 hours. Heat up briefly
to boiling point. Cover, cool to 75°F (24°C), and
stir in the rest of the ingredients. Maintain the
given temperature for 3 days, with frequent
stirring. Funnel into the fermentation jar, make
up to one gallon, fit the airlock, and maintain
the temperature.

Black Grape Jelly

Ingredients
Black grape jelly 2 lb
Honey ½ lb
Brown sugar ¼ lb
Citric acid 1 teaspoonful
Pectozyme 1 saltspoonful
Tea ¼ pint
Yeast nutrient 1 tablet
3 mg vitamin B1 tablet
Bordeaux yeast 1 tablet
Water to 1 gal

Method
Prepare the invert sugar, the tea, and the yeast
starter. Cover the jelly with boiling water and stir
in, cover, and cool to 60°F (16°C). Stir in the
pectozyme and the acid, cover, and leave for
24 hours. Heat up briefly to boiling point. Simmer
the honey in water for 15 minutes and pour onto
the liquid jelly contained in the bucket. Cover,
and cool to 75°F (24°C). Stir in the rest of the
ingredients, cover, and maintain the temperature
for 3 days, with frequent stirring. Funnel into the
fermentation jar, make up to one gallon, fit the
airlock, and maintain the given temperature.

Bramble Jam

Ingredients
Bramble jam $3\frac{1}{2}$ lb
Tea $\frac{1}{2}$ pint
Citric acid $\frac{1}{2}$ teaspoonful
Pectozyme $\frac{1}{2}$ teaspoonful
Yeast nutrient 1 tablet
3 mg vitamin B1 tablet
Burgundy yeast 1 tablet
Water to 1 gal

Method
Prepare the yeast starter and the tea. Stir boiling
water onto the jam contained in a bucket, strain
into a second bucket, cover and cool to 60°F
(16°C). Stir in the pectozyme and acid, cover,
and leave for 24 hours. Heat up briefly to boiling
point, cover and cool to 75°F (24°C). Stir in the
other ingredients, cover, and maintain the given
temperature for 3 days, with frequent stirring.
Funnel into a fermentation jar, make up to one
gallon, fit the airlock, and maintain the
temperature.

Carob Bean

Ingredients
Carob Beans 2 oz
Teabags 8
Brown sugar 2 lb
Citric acid 1 teaspoonful
Yeast nutrient 1 tablet
3 mg vitamin B1 tablet
G.P. wine yeast 1 tablet
Water to one gallon

Method
Prepare the invert sugar and the yeast starter.
Pour boiling water over the carob beans
(contained in a closed filter bag) and over the
teabags, cover, and cool to 75°F (24°C). Remove
the teabags and the carob beans. Stir in the
rest of the ingredients, cover, and maintain the
temperature for 3 days, stirring daily. Funnel into
the fermentation jar, make up to one gallon,
fit the airlock, and maintain the given temperature.

Carrot Juice

Ingredients
Carrot juice 20 fl oz bottle
Elderflowers, dried, ½ oz
Red grape concentrate 8 fl oz
Sugar 1½ lb
Citric acid 1 dessertspoonful
Tea ½ pint
Yeast nutrient 1 tablet
3 mg vitamin B1 tablet
G.P. yeast 1 tablet
Water to 1 gal

Method
Prepare the invert sugar, the tea, and the yeast
starter. Put the elderflowers in a filter bag closed

at both ends, pour boiling water over them, cover, and cool to 75°F (24°C). Remove the filter bag, stir in the other ingredients, and maintain at the given temperature for 3 days, stirring daily. Strain, funnel into the fermentation jar, make up to one gallon with cool boiled water, fit the fermentation lock, and maintain the given temperature.

Celery Juice

Ingredients
Celery (Celeriac) root juice 20 fl oz bottle
White grape concentrate 8 fl oz
Citric acid 1 dessertspoonful
Tea ½ pint
Sugar 1½ lb
Yeast nutrient 1 tablet
3 mg vitamin B1 tablet
G.P. yeast 1 tablet
Water to 1 gal

Method
Prepare the invert sugar, the tea, and the yeast starter. Stir everything together in the bucket, cover, and maintain a temperature of 70°F (21°C) for 3 days, with frequent stirring. Funnel into the fermentation jar, top up to one gallon, and maintain the given temperature.

Chamomile Tea Cubes

Ingredients
Chamomile tea cubes, pkt of 8 (2 oz)
White grape concentrate 12 fl oz
Citric acid 1 dessertspoonful
Tea ¼ pint
Sugar 1¼ lb

Yeast nutrient 1 tablet
3 mg vitamin B1 tablet
G.P. yeast 1 tablet
Water to 1 gal

Method
Invert the sugar and prepare the tea and the
yeast starter. Pour boiling water onto the tea
herb cubes in the bucket. Cover, and cool to
70°F (21°C). Stir in the other ingredients, cover,
and maintain the temperature for 3 days,
stirring daily. Funnel into the fermentation jar,
make up to one gallon with cool boiled water,
fit the airlock, and maintain the given
temperature.

Chestnut Purée

Ingredients
Chestnut purée 15½ oz tin
Malt extract 1 lb
Citric acid 1 teaspoonful
Sugar 1¼ lb
Amylozyme 1 dessertspoonful
3 mg vitamin B1 tablet
Burgundy yeast 1 tablet
Water to 1 gal

Method
Invert the sugar and prepare the yeast starter.
Gradually pour boiling water onto the purée
and malt extract contained in a bucket, stirring
to dissolve. Cover, cool to 75°F (24°C), stir in the
other ingredients, cover, and keep at this
temperature for 3 days, stirring twice daily.
Funnel into the fermentation jar, make up to one
gallon with cool boiled water, fit the airlock and
maintain the temperature.

Coffee

Ingredients
Instant coffee granules 2 oz
Malt extract ½ lb
Sugar 1¾ lb
Citric acid 1 teaspoonful
Yeast nutrient 1 tablet
3 mg vitamin B1 tablet
G.P. wine yeast 1 tablet
Water to 1 gal

Method
Invert the sugar and prepare the yeast starter.
Pour boiling water onto the coffee and extract
contained in a bucket, stir thoroughly, cover,
and cool to 75°F (24°C). Stir in the remaining
ingredients, cover, and maintain the temperature
for 3 days, skimming and stirring twice daily.
Funnel into the fermentation jar, make up to one
gallon, fit the airlock, and maintain the
temperature.

Cranberry-Burgundy Liqueur Preserve

Ingredients
Cranberry-Burgundy liqueur preserve 1 lb
Red grape concentrate 12 fl oz
Sugar ¾ lb
Tea ¼ pint
Citric acid 1 teaspoonful
Yeast nutrient 1 tablet
3 mg vitamin B1 tablet
Burgundy yeast 1 tablet
Water to 1 gal

Method
Invert the sugar, prepare the yeast starter and the
tea. Stir the preserve into cool boiled water, and

then the rest of the ingredients. Cover, and keep
at 75°F (24°C) for 3 days, stirring daily. Strain into
a fermentation jar, make up to one gallon, fit the
airlock, and maintain the temperature.

Ginger (1)

Ingredients
Root Ginger 2 oz
Malt extract ½ lb
Sugar 1¾ lb
Citric acid 1 teaspoonful
Yeast nutrient 1 tablet
3 mg vitamin B1 tablet
G.P. yeast 1 tablet
Water to 1 gal

Method
Invert the sugar and prepare the yeast starter.
Simmer the bruised ginger, contained in a closed
filter bag, in water for ½ hour, and pour the
liquid onto the extract contained in a bucket,
stirring to dissolve. Cover and cool to 75°F
(24°C). Stir in the other ingredients, cover, and
maintain at this temperature for 3 days, stirring
twice daily. Funnel into the fermentation jar,
make up to one gallon with cool boiled water,
fit the airlock, and maintain at the given
temperature.

Ginger (2)

Ingredients
Root ginger, 1½ oz
Red grape concentrate 4 fl oz
Citric acid 1 teaspoonful
Tea ¼ pint
Sugar 1¾ lb
Yeast nutrient 1 tablet

3 mg vitamin B1 tablet
G.P. yeast 1 tablet
Water to 1 gal

Method
Invert the sugar and prepare the tea and the
yeast starter. Simmer the bruised root ginger in
a closed filter bag in water for ½ hour, pour into
a bucket, cover and cool to 75°F (24°C). Stir in
the other ingredients, and maintain this
temperature for 3 days, stirring daily. Funnel into
a fermentation jar, make up to one gallon with
cool boiled water, fit the airlock, and maintain
the given temperature.

Grapefruit Juice

Ingredients
Unsweetened grapefruit juice 20 fl oz can
Malt extract ½ lb
Sugar 1¾ lb
Yeast nutrient 1 tablet
3 mg vitamin B1 tablet
Tokay yeast 1 tablet
Water to 1 gal

Method
Invert the sugar and prepare the yeast starter.
Pour boiling water onto the extract in a bucket,
cover, and cool to 91°F (33°C), then stir in the
other ingredients, cover, and maintain this
temperature for 3 days, stirring daily. Funnel into
a fermentation jar, make up to one gallon, fit the
airlock, and maintain the given temperature.

Grapefruit Powder

Ingredients
Grapefruit powder 21 oz (8 pkts)
Sugar ½ lb

Tea $\frac{1}{4}$ pint
Citric acid 1 saltspoonful
Yeast nutrient 1 tablet
3 mg vitamin B1 tablet
G.P. yeast tablet
Water to 1 gal

Method
Invert the sugar and prepare the tea and the
yeast starter. Stir the powder into cool boiled
water contained in a bucket, together with the
other ingredients. Cover, and keep at 70°F (21°C)
for 3 days, stirring daily. Funnel into a
fermentation jar, make up to one gallon, fit the
airlock, and maintain the given temperature.

Honey-Whisky Liqueur Preserve

Ingredients
Honey-Whisky liqueur preserve 2 lb
Honey $\frac{1}{2}$ lb
Citric acid 1 tablespoonful
Tea $\frac{1}{2}$ pint
Yeast nutrient 1 tablet
3 mg vitamin B1 tablet
G.P. yeast 1 tablet
Water to 1 gal

Method
Prepare the yeast starter and the tea. Stir both
lots of honey into cool boiled water contained
in a bucket, add a Campden tablet, and keep
covered for 24 hours. Stir in the other ingredients,
cover, and keep at 70°F (21°C) for 3 days, stirring
daily. Funnel into a fermentation jar, make up to
one gallon, fit the airlock, and maintain the
given temperature.

Lemon Essence (1)

Ingredients
Lemon essence 1 fl oz
White grape concentrate 8 fl oz
Teabags 8
Sugar 1½ lb
Citric acid 1 saltspoonful
Yeast nutrient 1 tablet
3 mg vitamin B1 tablet
G.P. yeast 1 tablet
Water to 1 gal

Method
Invert the sugar and prepare the yeast starter.
Pour boiling water onto the teabags contained
in a bucket, cover, and cool to 70°F (21°C).
Remove the teabags. Stir in the other
ingredients, cover, and keep at this temperature
for 3 days, stirring daily. Funnel into a
fermentation jar, make up to one gallon, fit the
airlock, and maintain the given temperature.

Lemon Essence (2)

Ingredients
Lemon essence 1 dessertspoonful (10 cc)
Water 19 fl oz (555 cc)
Vodka, 100° proof, 7 fl oz (190 cc)

Method
Funnel the essence into a winebottle, followed
by the Vodka, and top up with water in which
half a Campden tablet has been dissolved.
Cork, mix, and keep for a day or two before
drinking.

Lemon Powder

Ingredients
Lemon powder 21 oz
Sugar $\frac{1}{2}$ lb
Tea $\frac{1}{4}$ pint
Citric acid 1 saltspoonful
Yeast nutrient 1 tablet
3 mg vitamin B1 tablet
G.P. yeast 1 tablet
Water to 1 gal

Method
Invert the sugar and prepare the tea and the
yeast starter. Stir the powder into cool boiled
water contained in a bucket, together with the
other ingredients. Cover, and keep at 70°F (21°C)
for 3 days, stirring daily. Funnel into a fermentation
jar, make up to one gallon, fit the airlock, and
maintain the given temperature.

Lemon Tea

Ingredients
Lemon Tea 5$\frac{1}{4}$ oz jar
Honey 2 lb
Citric acid 1 saltspoonful
Yeast nutrient 1 tablet
3 mg vitamin B1 tablet
G.P. yeast 1 tablet
Water to 1 gal

Method
Prepare the yeast starter. Pour boiling water onto
the tea and honey. Cover, cool to 70°F (21°C),
add a Campden tablet, and leave covered for
24 hours. Stir in the other ingredients, and keep
covered at the given temperature for 3 days,
stirring daily. Funnel into a fermentation jar,

make up to one gallon, fit the airlock, and
maintain the temperature.

Lime Tea Cubes

Ingredients
Lime tea cubes 2 oz (pkt of 8)
White grape concentrate 12 fl oz
Citric acid 1 dessertspoonful
Tea $\frac{1}{4}$ pint
Sugar $1\frac{1}{4}$ lb
Yeast nutrient 1 tablet
3 mg vitamin B1 tablet
G.P. yeast 1 tablet
Water to 1 gal

Method
Invert the sugar and prepare the tea and the
yeast starter. Pour boiling water onto the lime
cubes contained in a bucket. Cover, and cool to
70°F (21°C). Stir in the other ingredients, cover,
and maintain the temperature for 3 days, stirring
daily. Funnel into a fermentation jar, make up to
one gallon with cool boiled water, fit the
airlock, and maintain the given temperature.

Malt Extract

Ingredients
Malt extract 1 lb
Sugar $1\frac{1}{4}$ lb
Citric acid 1 tablespoonful
Yeast nutrient 1 tablet
3 mg vitamin B1 tablet
Tokay yeast 1 tablet
Water to 1 gal

Method
Invert the sugar and prepare the yeast starter.
Pour boiling water onto the extract contained in

a bucket, cover, and cool to 91°F (33°C). Stir in
the other ingredients, cover, and maintain the
temperature for 3 days, stirring and skimming
twice daily. Funnel into a fermentation jar, make
up to one gallon, fit the airlock, and maintain
the given temperature.

Spices and/or herbs, suspended in a muslin bag
in the bucket for the 3 days of fermentation,
can be used to vary the flavour, which otherwise
is an acquired taste.

Mint

Ingredients
Mint (dried) 1½ oz (fresh) 1½ pint of leaves
White grape concentrate 12 fl oz
Citric acid 1 dessertspoonful
Tea ½ pint
Sugar 1¼ lb
Yeast nutrient 1 tablet
3 mg vitamin B1 tablet
G.P. yeast 1 tablet
Water to 1 gal

Method
Invert the sugar, and prepare the tea and the
yeast starter. Pour boiling water over the mint
contained in a closed filter bag in the bucket –
a large glass marble in the mint bag will keep it
submerged. Cover, cool to 70°F (24°C), stir in
the other ingredients, cover, and maintain the
temperature for 3 days, stirring twice daily.
Funnel the liquid into a fermentation jar, make
up to one gallon with cool boiled water, fit the
airlock, and maintain the given temperature.

Morello Cherry Conserve

Ingredients
Morello cherry Conserve 3½ lb
Tea ½ pint

Citric acid 1 saltspoonful
Pectozyme 1 saltspoonful
Yeast nutrient 1 tablet
3 mg vitamin B1 tablet
Bordeaux yeast 1 tablet
Water to 1 gal

Method
Prepare the tea and the yeast starter. Pour
boiling water onto the conserve in a bucket,
cover, and cool to 60°F (16°C). Stir in the
pectozyme and acid, cover, and leave for 24
hours. Heat up briefly to boiling point, cover,
and cool to 70°F (21°C). Stir in the other
ingredients, cover, and maintain the temperature
for 3 days, stirring daily. Funnel into a
fermentation jar, make up to one gallon, fit the
airlock, and maintain the given temperature.

Orange Powder

Ingredients
Orange powder 21 oz
Sugar ½ lb
Tea ¼ pint
Citric acid 1 saltspoonful
Yeast nutrient 1 tablet
3 mg vitamin B1 tablet
Sauterne yeast 1 tablet
Water to 1 gal

Method
Invert the sugar and prepare the tea and the
yeast starter. Stir the powder into cool boiled
water contained in a bucket, together with the
other ingredients. Cover, and keep at 70°F (21°C)
for 3 days, stirring daily. Funnel into a
fermentation jar, make up to one gallon, fit the
airlock, and maintain the given temperature.

Orris Root

Ingredients
Orris root 1½ oz
Teabags 8
Sugar 2 lb
Citric acid 1 teaspoonful
Yeast nutrient 1 tablet
3 mg vitamin B1 tablet
G.P. wine yeast 1 tablet
Water to 1 gal

Method
Invert the sugar and prepare the yeast starter.
Pour boiling water over the Orris root
(contained in a closed filter bag) and teabags,
cover, and cool to 75°F (24°C). Remove the
teabags and the Orris root. Stir in the rest of the
ingredients, cover, and maintain the temperature
for 3 days, with frequent stirring. Funnel into a
fermentation jar, make up to one gallon, fit the
airlock, and maintain the given temperature.

Pineapple Powder

Ingredients
Pineapple powder 21 oz
Sugar ½ lb
Tea ¼ pint
Citric acid 1 teaspoonful
Yeast nutrient 1 tablet
3 mg vitamin B1 tablet
Graves yeast 1 tablet
Water to 1 gal

Method
Invert the sugar and prepare the tea and the
yeast starter. Stir the powder into cool boiled
water contained in a bucket, together with the
other ingredients. Cover, and keep at 70°F (21°C)

for 3 days, stirring daily. Funnel into a
fermentation jar, make up to one gallon, fit the
airlock, and maintain the given temperature.

Raspberry

Ingredients
Raspberry pie filling 2–14 oz cans
Sugar 1¾ lb
Tea ½ pint
Yeast nutrient 1 tablet
3 mg vitamin B1 tablet
G.P. yeast 1 tablet
Water to 1 gal

Method
Invert the sugar and prepare the tea and the
yeast starter. Pour boiling water onto the pie
filling contained in a bucket, cover and cool to
75°F (24°C), stir in the other ingredients, cover
and keep at this temperature for 3 days, stirring
twice daily. Funnel into a fermentation jar, make
up to one gallon with cool boiled water, fit the
airlock, and maintain the temperature.

Raspberry Diabetic Preserve

Ingredients
Raspberry diabetic preserve 3½ lb
Sugar 2 lb
Pectozyme 1 saltspoonful
Citric acid 1 saltspoonful
Tea ¼ pint
Yeast nutrient 1 tablet
3 mg vitamin B1 tablet
G.P. yeast 1 tablet
Water to 1 gal

Method
Invert the sugar and prepare the tea and the
yeast starter. Stir the preserve into boiling water,

cover, and cool to room temperature; stir in the
pectozyme and the acid, and leave covered for
24 hours. Bring briefly to boiling point, cover,
cool to 75°F (24°C), and stir in the other
ingredients. Cover, and keep at this temperature
for 3 days, stirring daily. Funnel into a
fermentation jar, make up to one gallon, fit the
airlock, and maintain the given temperature.

Rice

Ingredients
Rice 1½ lb (brown or red only)
Red grape concentrate 12 fl oz
Sugar 1¼ lb
Citric acid 1 tablespoonful
Amylozyme 1 dessertspoonful
Yeast nutrient 1 tablet
3 mg vitamin B1 tablet
G.P. yeast 1 tablet
Water to 1 gal

Method
Cover the unbroken whole rice with boiled water
cooled to room temperature, stir in the
amylozyme and the acid, together with 2 Campden
tablets, cover, and stir daily for 3 days. Prepare
the yeast starter and invert the sugar. Bring the
rice water briefly to boiling point, cover and
cool to 75°F (24°C). Stir in the other ingredients,
cover, and keep at 75°F (24°C) for 3 days, stirring
daily. Strain into a fermentation jar, make up to
one gallon with boiled and cooled water, fit the
airlock, and maintain the given temperature.

Rosehip Purée

Ingredients
Rosehip purée ½ (15 oz) can
Sugar 2 lb

Tea ½ pint
Citric acid 1 teaspoonful
Yeast nutrient 1 tablet
3 mg vitamin B1 tablet
Tokay yeast 1 tablet
Water to 1 gal

Method
Invert the sugar and prepare the tea and the
yeast starter. Put all the ingredients into a bucket,
stir, and keep covered at 75°F (24°C) for 3 days,
stirring daily. Strain into a fermentation jar,
make up to one gallon, fit the airlock, and
maintain the temperature. You'll gain a week if
you can keep the temperature at 91°F (33°C).

Rosehip Tea Cubes

Ingredients
Rosehip tea cubes 2 oz (pkt of 8)
Red grape concentrate 12 fl oz
Citric acid 1 dessertspoonful
Tea ½ pint
Sugar 1¼ lb
Yeast nutrient 1 tablet
3 mg vitamin B1 tablet
Sherry yeast tablet
Water to 1 gal

Method
Invert the sugar and prepare the household tea
and the yeast starter. Pour boiling water onto the
rosehip cubes in a bucket, cover, and cool to
75°F (24°C). Stir in the other ingredients, cover,
and maintain the temperature for 3 days, stirring
daily. Funnel into a fermentation jar, make up to
one gallon, fit the airlock, and maintain the given
temperature.

Rum Essence

Ingredients
Rum essence 1 fl oz
Red grape concentrate 8 fl oz
Teabags 8
Brown sugar $1\frac{1}{2}$ lb
Citric acid 1 teaspoonful
Yeast nutrient 1 tablet
3 mg vitamin B1 tablet
G.P. yeast 1 tablet
Water to 1 gal

Method
Invert the sugar and prepare the yeast starter.
Pour boiling water over the teabags, remove
them after 10 minutes, cover, and leave to cool
to 75°F (24°C) in the bucket. Stir in the rest of
the ingredients, make up to one gallon, and leave
covered for 3 days, maintaining the given
temperature and stirring daily. Funnel into the
fermentation jar, make up to one gallon, fit the
airlock, and maintain the temperature.

Tangerine Marmalade

Ingredients
Tangerine marmalade $3\frac{1}{2}$ lb
Rohament P 1 saltspoonful
Pectozyme 1 saltspoonful
Citric acid 1 saltspoonful
Tea $\frac{1}{4}$ pint
Yeast nutrient 1 tablet
3 mg vitamin B1 tablet
Chablis yeast 1 tablet
Water to 1 gal

Method
Prepare the yeast starter and the tea. Stir boiling
water into the marmalade in a bucket, cool to

room temperature, stir in the rohament, pectozyme and acid, and leave covered for 24 hours.
Bring briefly to boiling point, cover and cool to 70°F (21°C), and stir in the other items. Keep covered at this temperature for 3 days, stirring daily. Syphon into a fermentation jar, make up to one gallon, fit the airlock, and maintain the given temperature.

Tomato

Ingredients
Tomato juice 1 lb 12 oz can
White grape concentrate 8 fl oz
Sugar 1½ lb
Tea ½ pint
Citric acid 1 dessertspoonful
Yeast nutrient 1 tablet
3 mg vitamin B1 tablet
G.P. yeast 1 tablet
Water to 1 gal

Method
Prepare the yeast starter and the tea; invert the sugar. Stir all the ingredients into a bucket, cover, and keep at 75°F (24°C) for 3 days, stirring twice daily. Strain and funnel into a fermentation jar, make up to one gallon, fit the airlock, and maintain the given temperature. Garnish the wineglassful with a bay leaf.

Vanilla Essence

Ingredients
Vanilla essence 1 fl oz
Honey 2½ lb
Teabags 8
Citric acid 1 teaspoonful
Yeast nutrient 1 tablet

3 mg vitamin B1 tablet
G.P. yeast 1 tablet
Water to 1 gal

Method
Invert the sugar and prepare the yeast starter.
Pour boiling water over the teabags, remove them
after 10 minutes, cover, and cool to 70°F (21°C)
in the bucket. Stir in the other ingredients, and
keep covered at this temperature for 3 days,
stirring daily. Funnel into a fermentation jar,
make up to one gallon, fit the airlock, and
maintain the temperature.

Vervain

Ingredients
Vervain tea cubes 2 oz (pkt of 8)
White grape concentrate 12 fl oz
Citric acid 1 dessertspoonful
Tea ½ pint
Sugar 1¼ lb
Yeast nutrient 1 tablet
3 mg vitamin B1 tablet
G.P. yeast 1 tablet
Water to 1 gal

Method
Invert the sugar and prepare the yeast starter,
also the household tea. Pour boiling water onto
the Vervain cubes in the bucket, cover, and
maintain the temperature for 3 days, stirring
daily. Funnel into a fermentation jar, make up to
one gallon, fit the airlock, and maintain the given
temperature.

Vin Blanc (1)

Ingredients
Pineapple juice 19½ fl oz can
White grape concentrate 8 fl oz

Sugar 1 lb
Citric acid 1 teaspoonful
Tea $\frac{1}{4}$ pint
Yeast nutrient 1 tablet
3 mg vitamin B1 tablet
G.P. yeast 1 tablet
Water to 1 gal

Vin Blanc (2)

Ingredients
White grape concentrate 2 lb 3 oz (27 fl oz)
Sugar 5 oz
Citric acid 1 teaspoonful
Yeast nutrient 1 tablet
3 mg vitamin B1 tablet
G.P. yeast 1 tablet
Water to 1 gal

Method
Prepare the yeast starter, the tea (recipe 1), and invert the sugar. Stir all the ingredients in a bucket, cover, and keep at 70°F (21°C) for 3 days, stirring daily. Funnel into a fermentation jar, make up to one gallon, fit the airlock and maintain the temperature.

Vin Rosé (1)

Ingredients
Rosehip syrup 12 fl oz bottle
White grape concentrate 4 fl oz
Sugar $\frac{1}{4}$ lb
Citric acid 1 dessertspoonful
Tea $\frac{1}{4}$ pint
Yeast nutrient 1 tablet
3 mg vitamin B1 tablet
G.P. yeast 1 tablet
Water to 1 gal

Vin Rosé (2)

Ingredients
Red grape concentrate 17 fl oz
Honey 1¼ lb
Citric acid 1 teaspoonful
Yeast nutrient 1 tablet
3 mg vitamin B1 tablet
G.P. yeast 1 tablet
Water to 1 gal

Method
Prepare the yeast starter, the tea (recipe 1),
and invert the sugar (recipe 1). Simmer the
honey for 15 min in water, stirring to prevent
burning, cover and cool to 70°F (21°C)
(recipe 2). Stir all the ingredients in a bucket,
cover, and keep at the given temperature for 3
days, stirring daily. Funnel into a fermentation
jar, make up to one gallon, fit the airlock, and
maintain the temperature.

Vin Rouge (1)

Ingredients
Blackcurrant syrup 12 fl oz bottle
Red grape concentrate 4 fl oz
Sugar 1¼ lb
Citric acid 1 saltspoonful
Tea 2 fl oz
Pectozyme 1 saltspoonful
Yeast nutrient 1 tablet
3 mg vitamin B1 tablet
G.P. yeast 1 tablet
Water to 1 gal

Vin Rouge (2)

Ingredients
Red grape concentrate 2 lb 3 oz (27 fl oz)
Sugar 5 oz

Citric acid 1 teaspoonful
Yeast nutrient 1 tablet
3 mg vitamin B1 tablet
G.P. yeast 1 tablet
Water to 1 gal

Method
Prepare the yeast starter, the tea (recipe 1),
and invert the sugar. Stir the pectozyme and the
acid into the syrup and half the water, leave
covered at room temperature for 24 hours, bring
briefly to boiling point, cover and cool to 75°F
(24°C) (recipe 1). Stir all the ingredients in a
bucket, cover, and keep at the given
temperature for 3 days, stirring daily. Funnel into
a fermentation jar, make up to one gallon, fit the
airlock, and maintain the temperature.

Wheat

Ingredients
Wheat 1 lb
Red grape concentrate 16 fl oz
Amylozyme 1 dessertspoonful
Tea ½ pint
Citric acid 1 dessertspoonful
Brown sugar 1 lb
Yeast nutrient 1 tablet
3 mg vitamin B1 tablet
Cereal yeast 1 tablet
Water to 1 gal

Method
Invert the sugar, and prepare the tea and the
yeast starter. Soak the wheat overnight, mince
and return to the liquor, pour boiling water over
it, cool to room temperature, stir in the
amylozyme and acid, cover, and leave for 24
hours. Strain into a bucket, stir in the other

ingredients, cover, and keep at 75°F (24°C) for
3 days, stirring daily. Funnel into a fermentation
jar, make up to one gallon, fit the airlock, and
maintain the temperature.

WINE COCKTAILS – for formal entertaining

Bilberry Champagne

Ingredients
Bilberry Pie Filling Wine (described later)
Sugar 1 cube
Angostura Bitters
Lemon Peel

Method
Put the lump of sugar into a cocktail glass
(capacity 3 fl oz), and soak it with Angostura
Bitters. Add three squeezes of lemon juice.
Top up with ice-cold Bilberry Champagne, and
garnish with a small piece of lemon peel.

Damson Port

Ingredients
Damson Jam Wine (described later)
Unsweetened Orange Juice
Orange peel
Bilberry pie filling wine (described later)

Method
Put equal parts of the Damson Wine, orange
juice, and ice-cold Bilberry wine into a cocktail
glass, and garnish with a small piece of orange
peel.

Prune Sherry

Ingredients
Prune wine (described later)
Orange bitters

Method
Three parts fill the cocktail glass with prune wine,
and add a couple of dashes of orange bitters.

CORDIALS – stimulating warmers for cold days

Blackberry

Ingredients
Blackberry juice 1 quart
Sugar 1 lb
Cloves $\frac{1}{4}$ oz
Cinnamon $\frac{1}{4}$ oz
Nutmegs 2
Brandy $\frac{1}{4}$ bottle (7 fl oz)

Method
Gradually stir in the sugar while heating up the
juice, and skim off the scum after boiling point
has been reached; add the cloves, cinnamon and
grated nutmeg, and keep at simmering point for
30 minutes. Cover, and leave to cool. Funnel the
Brandy into a quart bottle, add the juice, and
stopper securely.

Peppermint

Ingredients
Peppermint tea cubes 4 oz (2 pkts of 8)
Sugar $\frac{1}{4}$ lb
Citric acid 1 dessertspoonful
Tea $\frac{1}{2}$ pint
Yeast nutrient 1 tablet
3 mg vitamin B1 tablet
G.P. yeast 1 tablet
Water to 1 gallon

Method
Invert the sugar, prepare the tea and the yeast
starter. Pour boiling water onto the herb tea

cubes in the bucket, cover, and cool to 75°F
(24°C). Stir in the other ingredients, cover, and
maintain the temperature for 3 days, stirring daily.
Funnel into the fermentation jar, make up to one
gallon, fit the airlock, and maintain the given
temperature.

CUPS AND COOLERS – for sportsmen and women

Burgundy

Ingredients
Victoria plum wine (described later) 1 bottle
Mineral water 1 quart bottle
Lemon 1
Caster sugar $\frac{1}{4}$ lb
Cucumber, small piece
Borage 1 leaf
Orange 1
Raspberry syrup 1 tablespoonful

Method
Put the wine into a large jug, add the peel of the
orange (no pith), and the juice of the orange and
of the lemon. Stir in the sugar and the raspberry
syrup. Add the thinly sliced cucumber and the
leaf of borage. Keep in the refrigerator until
required, then add the mineral water. Serve with
ice cubes.

Champagne Cider

Ingredients
Champagne cider (described later) $1\frac{1}{2}$ bottles
Soda water 1 bottle
Lemons 3
Nutmeg 1 saltspoonful
Caster Sugar $\frac{1}{4}$ lb
Mixed fresh fruit, to taste.

Method
Put the juice of the lemons, and the peel (no pith)
from one lemon into a jug, stir in the sugar and
the grated nutmeg; leave covered for 2 hours.
Strain through fine nylon into a large jug, add the
champagne cider, stir in the soda water, and
garnish with mixed fruit in season. Serve with
ice cubes.

Ginger Soda

Ingredients
Ginger wine (described earlier) 2 bottles
Soda water 2 bottles
Tea 1 pint
Lemons 2
Oranges 4
Sugar $\frac{1}{4}$ lb

Method:
Use fresh tea; strain it (if not using a teabag)
over the sugar contained in a large jug, and stir
to dissolve. Cover, and leave to cool. Add the
juice of the lemons and oranges, followed by a
few ice cubes. Add the ginger wine and the soda
water just before serving. Garnish with sliced
oranges and lemons, together with a sprig of
mint.

Rhubarb Wine

Ingredients
Rhubarb wine (described later) 1 bottle
Pineapple 3 thick slices
Caster sugar 2 tablespoonfuls
Strawberries 12
Soda water 1 bottle

Method
Cut the pineapple into cubes, and put them in a
bowl, together with the strawberries, sugar, and

bottle of rhubarb wine, and keep in the
refrigerator. Pour in the soda water just
before serving.

PUNCHES – Fireside warmers when frost's
about

Ginger

Ingredients
Ginger wine (described earlier) 1 bottle
Pure orange juice 1 quart
Tea 2 teacupfuls
Caster sugar to taste

Method
Pour over ice in a bowl, and sweeten to taste.

Damson

Ingredients:
Damson jam wine (described later) 1½ bottles
Orange 1
Cloves 20
Brown sugar

Method
Stick the cloves into the orange, and roll it in the
sugar. Roast in a slow oven until moderately
browned. Cut up, and simmer in a saucepan with
the wine for ¼ hour. Strain, when somewhat
cooler, into the warmed bowl. Sweeten with the
sugar to taste.

Redcurrant

Ingredients
Redcurrant jelly wine (described later) 1 bottle
Angostura bitters 20 dashes

Caster sugar 1 oz.
Cinnamon 9 in stick
Cloves 3
Allspice 5 teaspoonfuls
Lemon peel from one lemon

Method
Put the ingredients into a saucepan, place on a
source of heat, and remove just before boiling
point. Strain, when cooled a little, into the warmed
bowl.

APERITIF – to whet the appetite

Banana

Ingredients
Bananas, dried $\frac{1}{4}$ lb (Fresh 1 lb)
White *or* red grape concentrate 8 fl oz
Sugar $2\frac{1}{4}$ lb
Citric acid 1 dessertspoonful
Tea $\frac{1}{2}$ pint
Yeast nutrient 1 tablet
3 mg vitamin B1 tablet
G.P. yeast 1 tablet
Water to 1 gallon

Method
Prepare the yeast starter, also the tea, and invert
the sugar. Cover the bananas with water in a
bucket, cover the bucket and leave for 24 hours,
simmer for 5 minutes, strain into another bucket,
cover, and cool to 70°F (21°C). Stir in the other
ingredients, and keep at the given temperature
for 3 days, stirring daily. Funnel into a
fermentation jar, make up to one gallon, fit the
airlock, and maintain the temperature.
Can be given other aperitif flavours with the
addition of wine essences, ordinary essences,

herb essences, or by steeping coriander, cinnamon, cloves, orris root, or a special preparation of vermouth herbs in the wine, to taste. Use the grape concentrate which suits the colour of the additive.

Champagne Cider

Ingredients
Apple juice 6 pint
Sugar 1 lb
Citric acid 1 dessertspoonful
Pectozyme 1 dessertspoonful
Fungal amylase 1 saltspoonful
Yeast nutrient 1 tablet
3 mg vitamin B1 tablet
Champagne yeast 1 tablet
Water to 1 gallon

Method
Juice extractor owners will require at the least 10 lb of mixed dessert and cooking apples, and a Campden tablet will prevent discoloration of the juice as it is being extracted. If you buy the juice, add a Campden tablet as soon as you expose it to the air. Make the juice up to one gallon in a bucket, stir in the acid, fungal amylase and pectozyme, cover, and leave at room temperature for 24 hours, with frequent stirring. Bring briefly to 151°F. (66°C), and then stir in the inverted sugar, the nutrient, and vitamin tablet. (If you possess a beer mashing immersion heater, this is ideal for raising the temperature to the required level – higher temperatures may not improve the taste of this wine). Allow to cool to 70°F (21°C), stir in the yeast starter prepared two days previously, and keep covered at this temperature for 3 days, stirring twice daily. Funnel into a fermentation jar, make up to one

gallon, fit the airlock, and keep at the same
temperature until the fermentation has ceased;
this end point is important, and a "Clinitest"
proprietary sugar tester should be used. Syphon
into champagne (none other) bottles to within
3 in of the top of the neck, add $\frac{1}{2}$ fl oz (14 cc)
of cool sugar syrup (5 oz sugar dissolved in
3 fl oz water brought briefly to boiling point),
and $\frac{1}{4}$ fl oz (7 cc) of yeast starter. Keep at room
temperature until required for drinking, and then
in the refrigerator for an hour before serving.
The corks have to be wired down, of course.

Tea

Ingredients
Teabags 8
White *or* red grape concentrate 8 fl oz
Sugar 2$\frac{1}{4}$ lb
Citric acid 1 dessertspoonful
Yeast nutrient 1 tablet
3 mg vitamin B1 tablet
Tokay Yeast 1 tablet
Water to 1 gallon

Method
Invert the sugar and prepare the yeast starter.
Pour boiling water on to the teabags, cover, cool
to 70°F (21°C), remove the teabags, stir in the
other ingredients, cover, and keep at this
temperature for 3 days, stirring daily. Funnel into
the fermentation jar, make up to one gallon,
fit the airlock, and maintain the temperature.

Can be flavoured as described for banana
aperitif wine.

TABLE WINES – with hors d'oeuvre

Apple

Ingredients
Dried Apples ¼ lb
Dried bananas ¼ lb
Red grape concentrate 4 fl oz
Sugar 1¾ lb
Citric acid 1 dessertspoonful
Rohament P 1 saltspoonful
Pectozyme 1 saltspoonful
Yeast nutrient 1 tablet
3 mg vitamin B1 tablet
Sherry yeast 1 tablet
Water to 1 gallon

Method
Invert the sugar and prepare the yeast starter.
Put the apples, bananas, acid, rohament and
pectozyme into a bucket, cover with tapwater,
cover the bucket, and keep at room temperature
for 24 hours, stirring frequently. Bring to the boil
briefly, pour through a canvas filter bag into a
bucket, expressing the juice. Cover, cool to 75°F
(24°C), stir in the other ingredients, cover, and
keep at this temperature for 3 days, stirring daily.
Funnel into a fermentation jar, make up to one
gallon, fit the airlock, and maintain the
temperature.

Gooseberry

Ingredients
Gooseberries 20.2 fl oz can
White grape concentrate 8 fl oz
Elderflowers, dried ¾ oz (Fresh, ¾ pint)
Sugar 1¼ lb
Tea ½ pint

Rohament P 1 saltspoonful
Pectozyme 1 saltspoonful
Yeast nutrient 1 tablet
3 mg vitamin B1 tablet
G.P. yeast 1 tablet
Water to 1 gallon

Method
Prepare the yeast starter and the tea, and invert
the sugar. Pour the gooseberries into a bucket,
sprinkle on the rohament and pectozyme, cover,
and keep at room temperature for 24 hours,
stirring frequently. Bring briefly to boiling point,
pour through a canvas filter bag into a bucket,
expressing the juice, cover, cool to 70°F (21°C),
stir in the other ingredients, cover, and maintain
the temperature for 3 days, stirring twice daily.
Strain and funnel into a fermentation jar, make up
to one gallon, fit the airlock, and maintain the
temperature.

Sherry

Use sherry grape juice concentrate to the
previously given Vin Blanc (2) recipe; this wine
is favoured dry.

TABLE WINES – with oysters and shellfish

Dandelion

Ingredients
Dandelions, dried 2 oz (Fresh 1 quart)
White grape concentrate 16 fl oz
Honey 1½ lb
Tea ½ pint
Citric acid 1 dessertspoonful
3 mg vitamin B1 tablet
Yeast nutrient 1 tablet

Graves yeast 1 tablet
Water to 1 gallon

Method
Prepare the yeast starter and the tea. Stir the
honey into boiling water, cool to 70°F (21°C), stir
in the other ingredients, keep at this
temperature for 3 days, stirring twice daily.
Strain, funnel into the fermentation jar, make up
to one gallon, fit the airlock, and maintain the
temperature.

Graves

Use graves grape juice concentrate to the
previously given Vin Blanc (2) recipe; this wine
is favoured dry.

Lime

Ingredients
Sugar-free lime marmalade 3½ lb
Honey 2¾ lb
Pectozyme 1 saltspoonful
Citric acid 1 dessertspoonful
Tea ½ pint
3 mg vitamin B1 tablet
Yeast nutrient 1 tablet
Burgundy yeast 1 tablet
Water to 1 gallon

Method
Prepare the yeast starter and the tea. Stir the
honey into boiling water, pour over the
marmalade contained in a bucket, cover, cool to
70°F (21°C), stir in the acid and pectozyme, cover,
leave for 24 hours, bring briefly to boiling point,
cover and cool to the given temperature. Stir in
the other ingredients, cover, keep at this

temperature for 3 days, stirring daily. Strain and funnel into a fermentation jar, make up to one gallon, fit the airlock, and maintain the temperature.

TABLE WINES – with soup

Greengage

Ingredients
Greengage jam 3¼ lb
White grape concentrate 4 fl oz
Rohament P 1 saltspoonful
Pectozyme 1 saltspoonful
Citric acid 1 teaspoonful
Tea ¼ pint
3 mg vitamin B1 tablet
Yeast nutrient 1 tablet
Madeira yeast 1 tablet
Water to 1 gallon

Method
Prepare the yeast starter and the tea. Stir boiling water into the jam, cover, cool to room temperature, stir in the pectozyme, rohament and acid, cover, leave for 24 hours, bring briefly to boiling point, cover, cool to 70°F (21°C), stir in the other ingredients, and keep covered at this temperature for 3 days, stirring daily. Strain and funnel into the fermentation jar, make up to one gallon, fit the airlock, and maintain the temperature.

Madeira

Use Madeira grape juice concentrate to the previously given Vin Rouge (2) recipe; this wine is favoured dry.

Malaga

Use Malaga grape juice concentrate to the
previously given Vin Blanc (2) recipe; this wine
is favoured medium-dry.

Orange Juice

Ingredients
Unsweetened orange juice $19\frac{1}{2}$ fl oz can
Sultanas $\frac{1}{2}$ lb
Sugar $1\frac{3}{4}$ lb
Tea $\frac{1}{2}$ pint
Citric acid 1 saltspoonful
Rohament P 1 saltspoonful
3 mg vitamin B1 tablet
Yeast nutrient 1 tablet
Sherry yeast 1 tablet
Water to 1 gallon

Method
Invert the sugar, prepare the yeast starter and the
tea. Mince the sultanas, cover with boiling water,
cover the bucket, cool to room temperature, stir
in the acid and rohament, cover, and after 24
hours bring briefly to the boil and express
through a canvas filter bag. Cool to 75°F (24°C),
stir in the other ingredients, and maintain this
temperature for 3 days, stirring daily. Funnel into
a fermentation jar, make up to one gallon, fit the
airlock, and maintain the temperature.

TABLE WINES – with egg dishes

Burgundy

Use White Burgundy grape juice concentrate to
the previously given Vin Blanc (2) recipe; this
wine is favoured dry.

Orange

Ingredients
Sweetened orange juice 25½ fl oz can
White grape concentrate 8 fl oz
Elderflowers, dried ½ oz (Fresh ½ pint)
Honey 1½ lb
Tea ¼ pint
3 mg vitamin B1 tablet
Yeast nutrient 1 tablet
Burgundy yeast 1 tablet
Water to 1 gallon

Method
Prepare the tea and the yeast starter. Stir the
honey into boiling water, cover and cool to
70°F (21°C). Stir in the other ingredients, cover,
and keep at this temperature for 3 days, stirring
twice daily. Strain into a fermentation jar, make
up to 1 gallon, fit the airlock, and maintain at the
given temperature.

TABLE WINES – with fish

Hock

Use hock grape juice concentrate to the
previously given Vin Blanc (2) recipe.

Peach

Ingredients
Sorbital sweetened peaches 19 fl oz can
Sugar 2 lb
Tea ¼ pint
Citric acid 1 dessertspoonful
Rohament P 1 saltspoonful
3 mg vitamin B1 tablet
Yeast nutrient 1 tablet

Graves yeast 1 tablet
Water to 1 gallon

Method
Prepare the yeast starter, also the tea, and invert
the sugar. Sprinkle rohament and the acid on the
opened can of peaches, cover, and leave at room
temperature for 24 hours. Bring briefly to boiling
point, express through a canvas filter bag into a
bucket, cover and cool to 70°F (21°C), stir in the
other ingredients, cover, and keep at this
temperature for 3 days, stirring daily. Funnel into
a fermentation jar, make up to one gallon, fit the
airlock, and maintain the temperature.

Rhubarb

Ingredients
Rhubarb 29.7 fl oz (2 cans)
Red grape concentrate 12 fl oz
Elderflower, dried ½ oz (Fresh ½ pint)
Sugar ¾ lb
Precipitated chalk 1 tablespoonful
Citric acid 1 dessertspoonful
Rohament P 1 saltspoonful
Tea ½ pint
3 mg vitamin B1 tablet
Yeast nutrient 1 tablet
Hock yeast 1 tablet
Water to 1 gallon

Method
Invert the sugar, prepare the tea and the yeast
starter. Sprinkle the chalk on to the rhubarb until
fizzing stops. Stir in the rohament and the acid,
cover, and leave for 24 hours. Bring briefly to
151°F (66°C) (do not boil), cover, and cool to
75°F (24°C). Stir in the other items, cover, and
keep at the given temperature for 3 days, stirring

frequently. Strain into a fermentation jar, make
up to one gallon, fit the airlock, and maintain
the temperature.

TABLE WINES – with entrées

Blueberry

Ingredients
Blueberry conserve 3½ lb
Citric acid 1 teaspoonful
3 mg vitamin B1 tablet
Yeast nutrient 1 tablet
Burgundy yeast 1 tablet
Water to 1 gallon

Method
Prepare the yeast starter. Stir boiling water into
the conserve, cover and cool to 75°F (24°C), stir
in the other ingredients, and keep at this
temperature for 3 days, stirring twice daily.
Strain into the fermentation jar, make up to one
gallon, fit the airlock, and maintain the
temperature.

Claret

Use claret grape juice concentrate to the
previously given Vin Rouge (2) recipe.

Redcurrant

Ingredients
Redcurrant jelly 3 lb
Red grape concentrate 4 fl oz
Tea ¼ pint
Citric acid 1 saltspoonful
Pectozyme 1 saltspoonful
3 mg vitamin B1 tablet

Yeast nutrient 1 tablet
Claret yeast 1 tablet
Water to 1 gallon

Method
Prepare the tea and the yeast starter. Dissolve
the jelly in hot water, cover, and cool to 75°F
(24°C). Stir in the acid and pectozyme, cover,
and leave for 24 hours. Bring briefly to boiling
point, cover, and cool to the given temperature.
Stir in the other ingredients, cover, and keep at
this temperature for 3 days, stirring daily.
Strain into a fermentation jar, make up to one
gallon, fit the airlock, and maintain the
temperature.

TABLE WINES – with roast

Burgundy

Use red burgundy grape juice concentrate to the
previously given Vin Rouge (2) recipe.

Elderberry

Ingredients
Elderberries, dried ½ lb
Raisins ½ lb
Sugar 1¾ lb
Citric acid 1 teaspoonful
3 mg vitamin B1 tablet
Yeast nutrient 1 tablet
G.P. yeast 1 tablet
Water to 1 gallon

Method
Invert the sugar and prepare the yeast starter.
Pour boiling water on to the elderberries and
minced raisins, cover, cool to 75°F (24°C), and stir

in the other ingredients. Cover, and maintain the
temperature for 3 days, stirring twice daily. Strain
into a fermentation jar, make up to one gallon,
fit the airlock, and maintain the temperature.

Victoria Plum

Ingredients
Victoria plum jam 3 lb
Red grape concentrate 4 fl oz
Citric acid 1 teaspoonful
Pectozyme 1 saltspoonful
3 mg vitamin B1 tablet
Yeast nutrient 1 tablet
Burgundy yeast 1 tablet
Water to 1 gallon

Method
Prepare the yeast starter. Stir the jam into
boiling water, cover and cool to 75°F (24°C).
Stir in the acid and pectozyme, cover, and leave
for 24 hours. Stir in the other ingredients, cover,
and maintain the given temperature for 3 days,
stirring twice daily. Strain into the fermentation
jar, make up to one gallon, fit the airlock, and
maintain the temperature.

TABLE WINES – with game

Beaujolais

Use Beaujolais grape juice concentrate to the
previously given Vin Blanc (2) recipe; best
appreciated medium-dry.

Elderberry

Ingredients
Elderberry juice ½ (15 oz) can
Red grape concentrate 4 fl oz

Sugar 1¾ lb
Citric acid 1 teaspoonful
3 mg vitamin B1 tablet
Yeast nutrient 1 tablet
Beaujolais yeast 1 tablet
Water to 1 gallon

Method
Prepare the yeast starter and invert the sugar.
Stir all the ingredients in a bucket, cover, and
keep at 75°F (24°C) for 3 days, stirring daily.
Funnel into the fermentation jar, make up to one
gallon, fit the airlock, and maintain the
temperature.

Pear

Ingredients
Sorbital sweetened pears 19 fl oz can
Sugar 2 lb
Citric acid 1 dessertspoonful
3 mg vitamin B1 tablet
Yeast nutrient 1 tablet
Champagne yeast 1 tablet
Water to 1 gallon

Method
Invert the sugar and prepare the yeast starter.
Crush the pears, and put everything into a
bucket, cover, and keep at 70°F (21°C) for 3 days,
stirring twice daily. Strain into a fermentation jar,
make up to one gallon, fit the airlock, and
maintain the temperature. Make the "Clinitest"
and proceed as for Champagne Cider previously
described.

DESSERT WINES—with sweets.

Bilberry

Ingredients
Bilberry Pie Filling 2 — 14 oz cans
White Grape Concentrate 4 fl oz
Sugar 1¾ lb
Citric Acid 1 teaspoonful
3 mg Vitamin B1 tablet
Yeast Nutrient 1 tablet
Champagne Yeast 1 tablet
Water to 1 gal.

Method
Invert the sugar and prepare the yeast
starter. Stir everything in a bucket, bring
to 70°F. (21°C), cover, and maintain the
temperature for 3 days, stirring twice daily.
Strain into a fermentation jar, make up to one
gallon, fit the airlock, and maintain the
temperature. Make the "Clinitest" and proceed
as for Champagne Cider previously
described.

Fig

Ingredients:
Figs 2 (15.5 fl oz) cans
Sugar 1¼ lb
Citric Acid 1 dessertspoonful
Tea ½ pint
3 mg. Vitamin B1 tablet
Yeast Nutrient 1 tablet
Tokay Yeast 1 tablet
Water to 1 gal

Method
Invert the sugar and prepare the tea and the
yeast starter. Squash the figs, and put all the

ingredients into a bucket, cover, and keep at
91°F (33°C) for 3 days, stirring twice daily.
Strain into a fermentation jar, make up to one
gallon, fit the airlock, and maintain the
temperature.

Peach

Ingredients
Dried Peaches 1 lb
Dried Bananas ¼ lb
Sultanas ¾ lb.
Honey 2 lb
Tea ¼ pint
Citric Acid 1 teaspoonful
3 mg Vitamin B1 tablet
Yeast Nutrient 1 tablet
Sauterne Yeast 1 tablet
Water to 1 gal

Method
Prepare the tea and the yeast starter. Simmer
the honey for 15 minutes in water, pour over the
dried fruit, squash, cover and cool to 70°F (21°C).
Stir in the other ingredients, cover, and
maintain the temperature for 3 days, stirring
frequently. Strain into a fermentation jar, make
up to one gallon, fit the airlock, and maintain
the temperature. Use 1½ oz glycerine for
maturation.

Port

Use Port Grape Juice Concentrate to the
previously given Vin Rouge (2) recipe;
this wine is favoured sweet.

DESSERT WINES — with cheese

Blackcurrant

Ingredients:
Blackcurrant Diabetic Preserve 5 lb
Brown Sugar 2 lb
Tea ¼ pint
Citric Acid 1 teaspoonful
Pectozyme 1 teaspoonful
3 mg. Vitamin B1 tablet
Yeast Nutrient 1 tablet
Port Yeast 1 tablet
Water to 1 gal

Method
Invert the sugar, prepare the tea and the
yeast starter. Pour boiling water over the
preserve, cover and cool to 75°F (24°C), stir in
the other ingredients, cover, and maintain the
temperature for 3 days, stirring twice daily.
Strain into a fermentation jar, make up to one
gallon, fit the airlock, and maintain the temperature.

Damson

Ingredients
Damson Jam 3 lb
Bananas 1 lb (Dried ¼ lb)
Elderflowers ¼ pint (Dried ¼ oz)
Red Grape Concentrate 8 fl oz
Pectozyme ½ teaspoonful
Citric Acid 1 teaspoonful
3 mg Vitamin B1 tablet
Yeast Nutrient 1 tablet
Port Yeast 1 tablet
Water to 1 gal

Method
Prepare the yeast starter. Stir boiling water
into the jam, bananas and flowers, cover, cool
to 75°F (24°C), and stir in the other
ingredients. Cover, keep at this temperature
for 3 days, stirring twice daily. Strain into a
fermentation jar, make up to one gallon,
fit the airlock, and maintain the temperature.

Prune

Ingredients
Prunes 2 lb
Sugar 1¼ lb
Tea ½ pint
Pectozyme 1 dessertspoonful
Citric Acid 1 desertspoonful
3 mg Vitamin B1 tablet
Yeast Nutrient 1 tablet
Sherry Yeast 1 tablet
Water to 1 gal

Method
Invert the sugar, prepare the tea and the
yeast starter. Pour boiling water onto the
prunes, squash to pulp, cover, and cool to 75°F
(24°C). Stir in the other ingredients, cover, and
maintain the temperature for 3 days, stirring
twice daily. Strain into a fermentation jar, make
up to one gallon, fit the airlock, and maintain
the warmth.

Sherry
Use Sherry Grape Juice Concentrate to the
previously given Vin Rouge (2) recipe; favoured
very sweet.

LIQUEURS — with coffee.

ESSENCE TYPE

Ingredients
Banana *or* Tea Aperitif Wines
with
Apricot Brandy Essence *or*
Curacao Essence *or*
French Vermouth Essence *or*
Peach Brandy Essence.

Method
In addition to the flavouring essence and the
wine (both of the wines are described on earlier
pages) we need some Vodka and some sugar
syrup with which to make our cut-price liqueurs.
A half-bottle of liqueur will probably satisfy most
needs.

A spirit or wine half-bottle contains 377 cc
(13.3 fl oz). Put $\frac{1}{2}$ teaspoonful, or $1\frac{1}{2}$ cc of the
flavouring essence (or the amount advised on
the bottle) into the spirit bottle, followed by
$87\frac{1}{2}$ cc (3 fl oz) of cold sugar syrup. The
syrup comes from your stock solution —
dissolve 2 lb. sugar to boiling point in 568 cc
(1 pint)of water, and store tightly corked.
Now add the amount of Vodka which is
required to give your 55° proof liqueur,
and top up with wine. Cork, shake to mix,
and the liqueur will be ready for drinking a week
later. Stir in a proprietary maturing agent if
desired.

If the Vodka is 100° proof, you need 180 cc
(6 fl oz). Using 140° proof Vodka,
120 cc (4 fl oz) is the amount needed.

PRESERVES TYPE

Ingredients
Honey-Whisky Preserve 1 lb
Water to 27 fl oz
Whisky ½ bottle

Method
Stand the jar of preserve in warm water, then
empty into a measuring jug. Stir in cool boiled
water to the 27 fl oz mark. Funnel 18 fl oz into a
spirit bottle, and the remainder into a half-bottle.
Top up both bottles with whisky, mix, and add
maturing agent if desired.

The same method can be used using Cherry-
Brandy Preserve and Brandy, and other ideas
on the same lines will readily spring to mind,
once the possibilities are appreciated.

STRAIGHT TYPE

Blackberry

Ingredients
Blackberries
Caster Sugar ½ oz
Cinnamon, small pinch
Cloves 1
Brandy

Method
Put the large, ripe, and cleaned blackberries
into a half-size spirit or winebottle, funnel the
sugar into the bottle, the cinnamon and cloves,
and fill up with brandy. Fit the stopper
and leave for 6 weeks. Strain through very
fine nylon, lightly pressing the fruit, and
re-bottle, adding a maturing agent if desired.

Caraway (Kummel)

Ingredients
Caraway Seeds ¼ oz
Brandy 10 fl oz
Sugar 1 oz
Water 3 fl oz

Method
Funnel the caraway seeds into a half-size wine
or spirit bottle, after bruising them in a mortar
with a pestle. Then funnel in the brandy. Put
the sugar and water into a small pan, bring
briefly to the boil, stirring to avoid burning,
cover, and leave to cool. Funnel into the
bottle and fit the cork. Strain through very fine
nylon after 5 weeks, and re-bottle for early
drinking.

Orange
Ingredients
Seville Orange, small
Cloves 2
Gin 10 fl oz
Sugar ½ lb
Water 4 fl oz

Method
Stick the cloves into the orange, put them in
a small jar, funnel in the gin, cover, and
leave for 4 weeks. Put the sugar and water into
a small pan, stir, while bringing to boiling point
briefly, cover, leave to cool, and funnel
into the jar. After 4 weeks, filter through
fine nylon, squeezing out the orange, and funnel
into a spirit half-bottle for drinking as
required.

Raspberry

Ingredients
Raspberries 5 oz
Brandy
Clove, small
Caster Sugar $\frac{3}{4}$ oz
Ratafia Essence 1 drop

Method
Put the cleaned raspberries into a half-bottle
with the clove, essence and sugar, and fill up
with brandy; add maturing agent, leave for
4 weeks tightly corked, strain and press
through very fine nylon, re-bottle and cork.
Drink as required.

For Grape Concentrate Enthusiasts

It has been described on earlier pages
how to make "quickie" grape concentrate
wines, and when you are thus armed with the
knowledge of how, with little trouble, to
have a bottle of wine ready for drinking at all
times, you will then wish to pursue the
ultimate objective of stocking your wine cellar
with bottles or casks in which wines of a
superior quality to your previously enjoyed
Vin Ordinaire types can be left to reach their
natural maturity. The actual time and work
involved in making these wines will not
be a great deal more than that spent
on your "Almost-Instant" Vin Ordinaire wines,
but it will be the waiting time before drinking
them which will test your patience.
When you buy some grape concentrate, it is
important to know its specific gravity.
Commercial fluids are supplied with this
information on the arbitrary degrees Baumé
scale, and if you are thinking of buying some
concentrate for which neither the specific
gravity nor the degrees Baumé reading is given,
then obtain this information before making your
purchase.
The degrees Baumé and the specific gravity
scales are related to the sugar content of the
concentrate, and may be tabulated as given
herewith.

Sugar Content of Grape Concentrates

Degrees Baumé	Specific Gravity	Sugar in 20 fl oz
20	1.160	7 oz
25	1.208	9 oz.
30	1.261	13 oz.
35	1.318	17 oz.
36	1.330	$17\frac{1}{2}$ oz.
37	1.343	18 oz.
38	1.355	19 oz.
39	1.368	$19\frac{1}{2}$ oz.
40	1.381	20 oz.
45	1.450	23 oz.
50	1.526	27 oz.
55	1.611	31 oz.

With the aid of this information, we can now proceed to formulate Aperitif, Table, Sparkling Table, Social, and Dessert wines, together with Liquers. Most grape juice concentrates are marketed at around 38° Baumé, or at a Specific Gravity of 1.355, and this is the standard concentration adopted throughout the following pages. The associated charts of grape concentrate and sugar requirements will enable you to make any required adjustment to the formulations in accordance with any marked difference in the specific gravity or degrees Baumé of the concentrate which you decide to use.

APERITIF

Grape Concentrate Requirement and Sugar Requirement Per Gallon of Wine

Degrees Baumé	Grape Concentrate	Sugar
20	80 fl oz	16 oz
25	60 fl oz	16 oz
30	45 fl oz	16 oz

Degrees Baumé	Grape Concentrate	Sugar
35	35 fl oz	16 oz
36	33 fl oz	16 oz
37	31 fl oz	16 oz
38	30 fl oz	16 oz
39	29 fl oz	16 oz
40	28 fl oz	16 oz
45	24 fl oz	16 oz
50	20 fl oz	16 oz
55	18 fl oz	16 oz

Standard Formulation
Grape Concentrate (38° Baumé) 30 fl oz
Sugar 1 lb
Yeast Nutrient 1 tablet
3 mg. Vitamin B1 tablet
Yeast 1 tablet
Water to 1 gall

Method
1. Sterilise all equipment.
2. Prepare the yeast starter.
3. Invert the sugar.
4. Pour the grape concentrate into a plastic bucket.
5. Stir in the water, cooled to 70°F. (21°C) for white wines and to 75°F (24°C) for red wines, also the inverted sugar, nutrient, vitamin tablet, and yeast starter. Maintain the required temperature for 7 days, stirring daily, and keep covered.
6. Syphon white wines into a fermentation jar, keeping the bottom end of the plastic tube at the bottom of the receiving vessel; funnel red wines into the fermentation jar. Top up to the neck of the jar with cool boiled water. Fit the bored bung and partly water-filled fermentation lock, and maintain the temperature and the water seal, rocking the jar occasionally.

7. If bubbling through the fermentation lock has not ceased after one month, syphon off (as previously described) into a clean, sterile fermentation jar, and refit the bung and fermentation lock. If necessary, repeat at monthly intervals. Save the first lot of sedimentary yeast in the refrigerator if making champagne.

8. When bubbling through the fermentation lock has ceased, make sure that all the sugar has fermented out by means of the Clinitest (a preparation sold at chemists for the use of diabetics so that they can check on the presence of unwanted sugar in their diets). Now syphon off from the sediment, and fine and filter cloudy wine (as previously described), or merely filter fairly clear wine to brilliance.

9. Syphon (as above-described) into the bottles; cork, capsule, label and date them. If making champagne, prepare a yeast starter from the refrigerated yeast 3 days before bottling time; champagne bottles, corks and wire must be used; add a level dessertspoonful of sugar (no more) and a teaspoonful of the yeast starter to each fully-fermented-out bottle of champagne before corking and wiring down. Keep at room temperature for a fortnight.

10. Do not mature white wines for longer than 12 months; red wines, 24 months.

11. Store champagne bottles so that the sediment lodges on the cork. Refrigerate before serving, remove the cork (practice and skill are required), re-cork and wire to warm a little before pouring into the glasses at around 41°F (5°C). The use of new champagne bottles, and a cloth to wrap around them, are an insurance against injury from explosion when handling champagne in the bottle.

Champagne

This celebration wine is a product of the upper reaches of the river Marne in northern France, where it is matured in the bottle for 2 years. It is usually a white wine, but some pink champagne is also made. It is the dry wine which is enjoyed as an aperitif. Use Champagne Grape Concentrate and a Champagne Yeast Starter in the standard Aperitif wine formulation.

Madeira

The island of this name, off the north-west coast of Africa, is where this wine originated. Its unique flavour comes from 6 months maturation in the cask at high temperature. It is made dry or medium-dry for drinking as an aperitif. The Sercial type is dry, the Verdelho medium-dry. Use Madeira Grape Concentrate and a Madeira Yeast Starter in the standard Aperitif wine formulation.

Port

Northern Portugal is the home of this wine. It is the White Port which is served, chilled, as an Aperitif. Use White Port Grape Concentrate and a Port Yeast Starter in the Standard Aperitif wine formulation.

Sherry

This wine comes from southern Spain. It is the pale, dry or very dry, Fino Sherry which makes a good Aperitif wine. The true quality wine is marked by the formation of a flor in the cask, which process is outside the scope of this book. Use Pale Sherry Grape Concentrate and a Sherry Yeast Starter in the standard Aperitif wine formulation.

Vermouth, French

This is a wine in which various aromatic fruits and herbs have been steeped; it originated from the desire to make wines spoilt by oxidation fit to drink. Wormwood has been used for centuries as a preservative in beer, now having been superseded by Hops, and its very bitter taste is masked in Vermouth by the other constituents. A well-known French Vermouth is Noilly Prat. Use French Vermouth Grape Concentrate and a Vermouth Yeast Starter in the standard Aperitif wine formulation.

Vermouth, Italian

The better-known Italian Vermouths are dry, white Martini and Cinzano, and their red counterparts. Use Italian Vermouth Grape Concentrate and a Vermouth Yeast Starter in the standard Aperitif wine formulation for these drinks, which are not only taken neat, but also with ice.

TABLE WINES

Grape Concentrate Requirement and Sugar Requirement Per Gallon of Wine

Degrees Baumé	Grape Concentrate	Sugar
20	70 fl oz	8 oz
25	50 fl oz	8 oz
30	40 fl oz	8 oz
35	30 fl oz	8 oz
36	28 fl oz	8 oz
37	26 fl oz	8 oz
38	25 fl oz	8 oz
39	25 fl oz	8 oz
40	24 fl oz	8 oz
45	21 fl oz	8 oz
50	18 fl oz	8 oz
55	16 fl oz	8 oz

Standard Formulation:
Grape Concentrate (38° Baumé) 25 fl oz
Sugar ½ lb
Yeast Nutrient 1 tablet
3 mg. Vitamin B1 tablet
Yeast 1 tablet
Water to 1 gal

Method
1. Sterilise all equipment.
2. Prepare the yeast starter.
3. Invert the sugar.
4. Pour the grape concentrate into a plastic
   bucket.
5. Stir in the water, cooled to 70°F. (21°C)
for white wines and to 75°F (24°C) for red
wines, also the inverted sugar, nutrient, vitamin
tablet, and yeast starter. Maintain the required
temperature for 3 days, stirring daily, and keep
covered.
6. Syphon white wines into a fermentation
jar, keeping the bottom end of the plastic
tube at the bottom of the receiving vessel;
funnel red wines into the fermentation jar.
Top up to the bottom of the neck of the jar with
cool boiled water. Fit the bored bung and
partly water-filled fermentation lock, and
maintain the temperature and the water seal,
rocking the jar occasionally.
7. If bubbling through the fermentation lock
has not ceased after one month (but it should
have ceased before that if a steady and full
temperature level has been maintained),
syphon off (as last described) into a clean and
sterile fermentation jar, and refit the
bung and fermentation lock.
If necessary, repeat at monthly intervals.
8. When bubbling through the fermentation
lock has ceased, make sure that all the sugar

has fermented out by means of the Clinitest. Now syphon off from the sediment, fining and mechanically filtering cloudy wine (as previously described), or merely put fairly clear wine through the mechanical filter in order to make it brilliantly clear.

9. Syphon (as described above) into the bottles; cork, capsule, label and date the bottles.

10. Do not mature white wines for longer than 12 months; red wines 24 months. The bottles of wine should be kept in a clean, adequately ventilated, dry and dark place which is not subject to extremes of temperature. A cupboard under the staircase, or a boxroom which satisfies these conditions, is all that is necessary; polystyrene ceiling tiles are a decorative insulation against heat and cold — a $\frac{1}{2}$ in. thickness of this material has the insulation value of an 11 in thick cavity brick wall. A constant temperature of 45-50°F (7-10°C) is ideal. White Table wines are best served at a temperature of 50°F., and the red at 64°F. (18°C).

Beaujolais, White & Red

These wines come from the Burgundy district of France, and the white is usually inexpensive but dependable; it is most acceptable with fish, and is a dry wine; the red wine goes well with meat and game. Use Beaujolais Grape Juice Concentrate and a Beaujolais Yeast Starter in the standard Table wine formulation.

Burgundy, White & Red.

These grape concentrates have been given the name of the French district which produces Chablis and Beaujolais wines, among others. All the white wines go well with fish; the red wines

with meat and game. They are at their best dry.
Use Burgundy Grape Concentrate and a Burgundy
Yeast Starter in the standard Table wine
formulation.

Chablis
This is a very dry white wine from the Burgundy
district of France, and consequently goes
well with fish dishes. Use Chablis Grape
Concentrate and a Chablis Yeast Starter in the
standard Table wine formulation.

Chianti
Comes from Tuscany in Italy, and is a dry
red wine, best served with entrées. Use Chianti
Grape Concentrate and a Chianti Yeast
Starter, otherwise a G.P. Yeast Starter, in
the standard Table wine formulation.

Claret
This is reputed to be the supreme red wine
of France, and comes from the Medoc
district, north of Bordeaux, in the
south-west. It is best made dry, and is favoured
to accompany entrées and red meat. Use Claret
Grape Concentrate and a Claret Yeast Starter
in the standard Table wine formulation.

Graves
A dry white wine from the Bordeaux area of
France, which goes well with oysters and
fish dishes. Use Graves Grape Concentrate and
a Graves Yeast Starter in the standard Table
wine formulation.

Hock
From the Rhine regions in Germany, this fairly
dry white wine goes well with fish dishes.
Use Hock Grape Concentrate and a Steinberg

Yeast Starter in the standard Table wine
formulation.

Liebfraumilch
This grape concentrate carries the general
name given to cheap German Rhine district
wines, and is a dry white wine. Yeast
of the same name is available for making
Liebfraumilch wine, which will be to the
standard Table wine formulation.

Madeira
Made dry or medium-dry to accompany soup.
Use Madeira Grape Concentrate and a Madeira
Yeast Starter in the standard Table wine
formulation.

Marsala
This is a golden coloured wine from Sicily
which is best, and excellent served with the
soup course. It is not an expensive wine.
Use Marsala Grape Concentrate and a G.P.
Yeast Starter in the standard Table wine
formulation.

Riesling
This is a grape concentrate named after the
grape from which some German dry white
wines are fermented. Use a Riesling Yeast
Starter in the standard Table wine recipe.

Sherry
The table wine of this description is known as
Amontillado Sherry, and is full-coloured with
good body, medium-dry. It marries well with
shellfish, particularly lobster. Use the appropriate grape concentrate and yeast
starter in the standard Table wine recipe.

SPARKLING TABLE WINES

Grape Concentrate Requirement and Sugar Requirement Per Gallon of Wine

Degrees Baumé	Grape Concentrate	Sugar
20	80 fl oz	12 oz
25	60 fl oz	12 oz
30	45 fl oz	12 oz
35	35 fl oz	12 oz
36	33 fl oz	12 oz
37	31 fl oz	12 oz
38	30 fl oz	12 oz
39	29 fl oz	12 oz
40	28 fl oz	12 oz
45	24 fl oz	12 oz
50	20 fl oz	12 oz
55	18 fl oz	12 oz

Standard Formulation

Grape Concentrate (38° Baumé) 30 fl oz
Sugar ¾ lb
Yeast Nutrient 1 tablet
3 mg Vitamin B1 tablet
Yeast 1 tablet
Water to 1 gal

Method
1. Sterilise all equipment.
2. Prepare the yeast starter.
3. Invert the sugar.
4. Pour the grape concentrate into a plastic bucket.
5. Stir in the water, cooled to 70°F (21°C), also the inverted sugar, nutrient, vitamin tablet, and yeast starter. Maintain this temperature for 5 days, stirring daily, and keep covered.
6. Syphon into a fermentation jar, keeping the bottom end of the plastic tube at the bottom of the receiving vessel; top up to the neck of the

jar with cool boiled water. Fit the bored bung
and partly water-filled fermentation lock, and
maintain the temperature, together with the
water seal in the fermentation lock
(which can evaporate out on occasion), rocking
the jar occasionally.

7. If bubbling through the fermentation lock
has not ceased after one month, syphon off
(as described above) into a clean and sterile
fermentation jar, and refit the bung and partly
water-filled fermentation lock. Repeat at monthly
intervals if such is necessary. Save the first
lot of sedimentary yeast which was left behind
in the first fermentation jar.

8. When bubbling through the fermentation
lock has ceased, make sure that all the sugar
has fermented out, otherwise you will later run
the risk of bursting champagne bottles, which
can be dangerous. This is done by means of
the Clinitest. If sugar is still present, the
fermentation must be continued, as described
above-. Now syphon off from the
sediment, and fine and filter cloudy wine
(as previously described), or merely filter clear
wine to make it brilliantly clear.

9. Prepare a yeast starter from the
refrigerated yeast 3 days before bottling time.
The wine will be kept under the fermentation
lock, topped up to the neck of the
fermentation jar with boiled cool water, until
required for bottling.   Champagne bottles,
corks and wire, must be used, for safety
reasons, as previously mentioned; new ones are
best, but the judicious use of a blanket or such
will offer protection from bursting bottles. Add
a level dessertspoonful of sugar (no more),
and a teaspoonful of the yeast starter, to each
fully-fermented-out bottle of champagne, and
fill with the wine to within $2\frac{1}{2}$ in of the top of

the bottle neck, cork and wire down.
Keep at room temperature for a fortnight.

10. Store so that the yeast sediment can collect on the cork, and at a temperature of around 50°F (10°C). The wine should clear after about a couple of months, and if the wine is refrigerated before serving, the cork can be removed without too much spillage, after a considerable amount of practice, so that the sediment is disgorged. The cork and wire are then replaced to allow the champagne to acquire its full bouquet at a serving temperature of around 41°F (5°C).

Champagne
Best made dry for the table. Use Champagne Grape Concentrate and a Champagne Yeast Starter in the standard Sparkling Table wine formulation.

Pink Champagne
Use equal parts of Rosé and Champagne Grape Concentrates, together with a Champagne Yeast Starter in the standard Sparkling Table wine formulation.

SOCIAL WINES

Grape Concentrate Requirement and Sugar Requirement Per Gallon of Wine

Degrees Baumé	Grape Concentrate	Sugar
20	110 fl oz	6 oz
25	85 fl oz	6 oz
30	60 fl oz	6 oz
35	45 fl oz	6 oz
36	43 fl oz	6 oz
37	41 fl oz	6 oz
38	40 fl oz	6 oz
39	39 fl oz	6 oz
40	38 fl oz	6 oz

Degrees Baumé	Grape Concentrate	Sugar
45	33 fl oz	6 oz
50	28 fl oz	6 oz
55	25 fl oz	6 oz

Standard Formulation
Grape concentrate (38° Baumé) 40 fl oz
Sugar 6 oz
Yeast nutrient 1 tablet
3 mg vitamin B1 tablet
Yeast 1 tablet
Water to 1 gallon

Method
1. Sterilise all equipment.
2. Prepare the yeast starter.
3. Invert the sugar.
4. Pour the grape concentrate into a plastic bucket.
5. Stir in the water, cooled to 91°F (33°C), also the inverted sugar, nutrient, vitamin tablet, and Tokay yeast starter. Maintain this temperature for 7 days, stirring daily, and keep covered.
6. Syphon the white and rosé wines into a fermentation jar, keeping the bottom end of the plastic tube at the bottom of the receiving vessel; funnel the red wines into a fermentation jar. Top up to the neck of the jar, if necessary, with cool boiled water. Fit the bored bung and partly water-filled fermentation lock, and maintain the temperature, together with the water seal. Rock the jar occasionally.
7. If bubbling through the fermentation lock has not ceased after a fortnight, syphon off (as last described) into a sterile fermentation jar, and refit the bung and fermentation lock. If necessary, repeat at fortnightly intervals.
8. When bubbling through the fermentation lock has ceased, make sure that all the sugar has

fermented out by means of the Clinitest. Now syphon off from the sediment, fining and filtering cloudy wine (as previously described), and merely filtering wine which requires finishing to brilliance.
9. Syphon (as described above) into the bottles, cork, capsule, label and date them.
10. Do not mature the white wine for longer than 12 months; the red ones 24 months.

Red (Vin Rouge)
Most people prefer a dry wine. Use Red grape concentrate and a Tokay yeast starter in the standard social wine formulation.

Rosé (Vine Rosé)
Use the Rosé grape concentrate and the Tokay yeast starter in the standard social wine formulation.

White (Vin Blanc)
Use the white grape concentrate and a Tokay yeast starter in the standard social wine formulation.

DESSERT WINES

Grape Concentrate Requirement and Sugar Requirement Per Gallon of Wine

Degrees Baumé	Grape Concentrate	Sugar
20	140 fl oz	4 oz
25	105 fl oz	4 oz
30	75 fl oz	4 oz
35	57 fl oz	4 oz
36	54 fl oz	4 oz
37	52 fl oz	4 oz
38	50 fl oz	4 oz

Degrees Baumé	Grape Concentrate	Sugar
39	49 fl oz	4 oz
40	48 fl oz	4 oz
45	42 fl oz	4 oz
50	36 fl oz	4 oz
55	31 fl oz	4 oz

Standard Formulation
Grape concentrate (38° Baumé) 50 fl oz
Sugar $\frac{1}{4}$ lb
Yeast nutrient 2 tablets
3 mg vitamin B1 2 tablets
Yeast 1 tablet
Water to 1 gallon

Method
1   Sterilise all equipment.
2   Prepare the yeast starter.
3   Invert the sugar.
4   Pour 18 fl oz of the grape concentrate into a plastic bucket.
5   Stir in $5\frac{1}{2}$ pints of water, cooled to 70°F (21°C) for white wines, and to 75°F (24°C) for red wines, also the inverted sugar, nutrient, vitamins, and yeast starter. Maintain the required temperature for 4 days, stirring daily, and keep covered.
6   Syphon white wines into a fermentation jar, keeping the bottom end of the plastic tube at the bottom of the receiving vessel; funnel red wines into the fermentation jar. **Do not top up with water.** Fit the bored bung and part-water-filled fermentation lock, and maintain the temperature and water seal for 3 days, rocking the jar occasionally. Save the yeast deposit in a refrigerator if making champagne.
7   Funnel in 16 fl oz of grape concentrate, **do not top up with water**, refit the fermentation lock, and maintain the temperature for a further 3 days, again rocking the jar occasionally.

8   Funnel in the remaining 16 fl oz of grape concentrate, top up with cool boiled water to the bottom of the neck of the jar, if necessary, refit the fermentation lock, and maintain the temperature for a further 7 days, again rocking the jar occasionally.

9   Now syphon into another fermentation jar, discharging the syphon tube into a funnel placed in the neck of the jar, so that a cascade occurs. Top up with cool boiled water, if necessary, and refit the fermentation lock.

10   Repeat Stage 9 after a fortnight.

11   Repeat after a month.

12   If bubbling through the fermentation lock has not now ceased, repeat as necessary at monthly intervals.

13   When the bubbling has ceased, make sure that all the sugar has fermented out (this is particularly important in the case of champagne) by means of the Clinitest. Now syphon off from the sediment, making sure that none enters the plastic syphon tube, and fine and filter the wine if it is not clear, otherwise fairly clear wine need only be mechanically filtered to brilliance.

14   Syphon into the bottles, cork, capsule, label and date them. If making champagne, prepare a yeast starter from the refrigerated yeast 3 days before bottling time; champagne bottles, corks, and wire must be used, and they will preferably be new ones; on no account use bottles which are not perfectly sound. Add a level dessertspoonful of sugar (less rather than more if too great a gas pressure and the resultant danger is to be avoided) and a teaspoonful of yeast starter to each fully fermented-out bottle of champagne before corking and wiring down, together with a teaspoonful of lactose (unfermentable sugar). Keep at room temperature for a fortnight, so that the yeast can ferment the

added sugar and thus produce carbon dioxide
gas, which gives rise to the attractive bubbles in
your champagne glass.

15   Do not mature white wines for longer than
12 months; red wines for 24 months. You can
sample your table wines within 6 and 12 months
respectively, with every chance of satisfaction
with the end product.

16   Store champagne bottles so that the
sediment lodges on the cork. Refrigerate before
serving, remove the cork while holding the neck
pointing downwards, and re-cork and wire before
later pouring into the glasses at around 41°F
(5°C). If served straight from refrigeration, the
bouquet will suffer.

17   The sweetening of wines other than
champagne has been described previously.

Burgundy

This dry red wine is expected to be a good deep
colour, rich, and full-bodied when imbibed with
dessert foods. Use Burgundy grape concentrate
and a Burgundy yeast starter to the standard
Dessert wine formulation.

Champagne

This wine is normally made sweet for
complementing dessert. Use Champagne grape
concentrate and a Champagne yeast starter in the
standard formulation for a Dessert wine.

Hock

Make medium-dry with Hock grape concentrate
and a Steinburg yeast starter to the standard
Dessert wine formulation.

Madeira

Make sweet with Madeira grape concentrate and
a Madeira yeast starter to the standard Dessert

wine formulation. The Malmsey type is
dark-coloured, rich and full-bodied. Bual is
golden-coloured and full-bodied.

Malaga
This medium-sweet, golden coloured wine comes
from Malaga town in southern Spain. Use
Malaga grape concentrate and a G.P. yeast
starter to the standard Dessert wine formulation.

Muscat
A rich and dry white wine from France. Use
Muscat grape concentrate and a G.P. yeast
starter to the Dessert wine recipe.

Port
Full-bodied, medium-dry, rich and dark-red is the
Dessert type. Use red Port grape concentrate and
a Port yeast starter.

Sauternes
Chateau Yquem, the world's most famous
Dessert wine, is a sweet Sauternes from the
Bordeaux district of France. Use the named
concentrate and yeast to the Dessert wine recipe.

Sherry
The Dessert type is a sweet, rich, dark, heavy,
full-bodied Oloroso, of which the best known is
Bristol Cream. Use a Cream Sherry grape
concentrate and a Sherry yeast starter to the
standard dessert wine formulation.

LIQUEURS

To make grape concentrate liqueurs use a
light-flavoured Dessert wine, vodka, sugar and a
flavouring essence. The sugar is prepared by
dissolving 2 lb in one pint of water, bringing it

briefly to boiling point, covering and cooling.
How to make a spirit bottle of liqueur is
described, but you can reduce the given amounts
for sampling purposes. A graduated pipette,
of the type used with eye-drops, will measure
sample volumes, and a hydrometer jar graduated
in ccs. will enable you to repeat your favourite
recipes with greater accuracy. Put one
teaspoonful of flavouring essence into the bottle,
followed by 175 cc (6 fl oz) of cold sugar syrup.
Now add the amount of Vodka required to give
your chosen strength of liqueur, and in
accordance with the accompanying chart.
Top up with wine. Cork, shake to mix thoroughly,
and get out your liqueur glasses for use. If the
bottle of flavouring essence carries instructions
for the amount to use, follow such instructions,
the manufacturer knows the strength of his
goods better than his new customers; you can
later experiment to suit your own taste.

Degrees Proof Chart

			100° proof Vodka
Liqueur strength 30° proof			80 cc (7 fl oz)
,,	,,	40°	160 cc (10 fl oz)
,,	,,	45°	250 cc (14 fl oz)
,,	,,	55°	330 cc (18 fl oz)
			140° proof Vodka
Liqueur strength 30° proof			50 cc (4 fl oz)
,,	,,	40°	100 cc (7 fl oz)
,,	,,	45°	150 cc (9 fl oz)
,,	,,	55°	200 cc (12fl oz)